EUROCOUNSEL
SYNTHESIS
FINAL REPORT
PHASE 2

Counselling – a Tool for the Prevention and Solution of Unemployment

EF/94/09/EN

This report has been compiled by Glenys Watt, Director of Blake Stevenson Ltd. Glenys Watt has been the technical co-ordinator for the Eurocounsel programme since its inception in 1991, and prior to that undertook the research for the feasibility study.

Blake Stevenson Ltd is a research and consultancy company which specialises in social and economic development with a particular focus on issues relating to employment and unemployment.

European Foundation
for the Improvement of
Living and Working Conditions

EUROCOUNSEL
SYNTHESIS
FINAL REPORT
PHASE 2

Counselling – a Tool for the Prevention and Solution of Unemployment

by Glenys Watt

Loughlinstown House,
Shankill, Co. Dublin, Ireland
Tel.: +353 1 282 6888
Fax: +353 1 282 6456

Cataloguing data can be found at the end of this publication

Luxembourg: Office for Official Publications of the European Communities,
1994

ISBN 92-826-7868-7

Printed in Ireland

PREFACE

This report provides the results of the second phase of an action research programme entitled **EUROCOUNSEL** currently being undertaken by the Foundation. The aim of this programme is, through an interactive process of research, action and dialogue, to identify ways to improve the quality and effectiveness of information, advice, guidance and counselling services in relation to the prevention and solution of the problem of long-term unemployment.

As unemployment in most countries in Europe has risen during this period, it is evident that the aims of the programme as a whole have remained highly relevant. The importance of counselling, guidance, advice and information provision as tools to prevent and solve this problem have increasingly been recognised. Counselling is seen not only as an important element in the reintegration of the unemployed into the primary labour market but also in the wider context of avoiding social exclusion.

The Eurocounsel programme began in 1991 and the first phase involved action research in ten local labour market areas in six Member States. The aim of the first phase of work was to identify and assess the potential for the improvement of the quality and effectiveness of counselling services at their delivery point - the local level. During this phase local consultants collected and analyzed information about the provision of counselling within each of these ten areas, including discussion with the key actors in each area - public authorities, social partners, users of services and practitioners. Results from this first phase included an analysis of the key issues in relation to the framework of systems, access, process and outcomes.

While the first phase of Eurocounsel focused on the local labour market level, the second phase has sought to build transnational links and to increase dissemination and contact with other Member States. The local consultants continued during this phase to monitor and support developments in the local labour market areas. At the same time a portfolio of case studies of interesting and innovative practice was prepared and a number of elements of transnational contact undertaken. This last element included a meeting on issues arising from Eurocounsel for senior government officials; the organisation of a pilot programme of exchange visits for counselling practitioners; and a major international conference held at the Foundation's Conference Centre in Dublin in May 1993. These activities have resulted in the production of two further publications in addition to this report: the Portfolio of Case Studies of Interesting and Innovative Experience and the Eurocounsel Conference Report, "Improving Counselling Services for the unemployed and for those at risk of unemployment".

This Phase II report highlights a range of findings. These relate to the role of counselling in the light of rising unemployment and increasing pressure on resources. One area of concern is what counselling services are most appropriate in areas where there is low demand for labour; the report adds to the previously identified functions of counselling of solving, coping and prevention, a fourth - that of activating. A comprehensive model for counselling provision is suggested which depends on a more equal distribution of work and labour. Activation plays an important role if this model is to work. This relates to the recognition at European level of the need to find new ways to stimulate job creation within economic growth as described in the Commission of the European Communities' Employment Framework document in May 1993 and the White Paper on "Growth, Competitiveness, Employment" of December 1993. The report also makes further comments on issues of access, process and outcomes of counselling services. It concludes by making 15 recommendations which have emerged from the work during this second phase of the programme.

On 28 September 1993, this report was evaluated at a meeting of the Eurocounsel Advisory Committee on behalf of the Foundation's Administrative Board. The report was welcomed by the participants at this meeting. They felt it was a useful synthesis of the work to date and approved its publication.

The employers' representatives stressed their support for the Eurocounsel programme and emphasised the need to highlight the significance of counselling as a preventive mechanism. In this they saw the role of the social partners as a key one. There are no magic, quick fix solutions to unemployment, but counselling and guidance are important in resolving the problems. The UK government representative also felt the report was a useful one which brought out many of the issues currently being paid attention by his government. He raised also the key issue of resources for counselling and the importance of targeting. There was a need to draw in other resources, for example, from the social partners and the users themselves. There was agreement on the publication of the Phase 2 report and the case study portfolio, subject to some small amendments.

The participants then discussed the proposals of the third and final phase of the Eurocounsel programme. The framework proposed was accepted. The representative of the ILO stressed the increasing need for diversity (of services, of providers) to meet the complex and diverse needs of users in a changing labour market. The Foundation, he felt, should aim to identity a blueprint for counselling policy for the next decade. While the outcomes of counselling were difficult, if not impossible to measure, the participants believed that more attention should be paid to the issue of assessing quality and effectiveness. The Commission representative pointed to the increased importance of guidance and counselling in the Commission's own work. It will now form a part of all the major EU training programmes and the Foundation's work should feed EU into the Commission's work in this area. Good co-ordination with the Commission services and with CEDEFOP continue to be important for Eurocounsel.

The Foundation is now implementing the third phase of the Eurocounsel programme on the lines agreed with the Advisory Committee. Three key issues will be the subject of further research, namely the role of counselling linked to the creation of new employment opportunities, the question of the measurement of quality and effectiveness of counselling services, and the role of partnerships, intermediaries and alternative delivery systems. Some investigation will also be undertaken on the potential for the development of a European network in this area to further the exchange of information and experience. It is also proposed to widen the programme to include France and the Netherlands so as to provide an overview of developments in counselling provision in the light of the issues identified by Eurocounsel to date.

Dublin, April 1994

CONTENTS

LIST OF TABLES

1   INTRODUCTION

EUROCOUNSEL is an action research programme whose aim is to improve the quality and effectiveness of information, advice, guidance and counselling services in relation to the prevention and solution of long-term unemployment. It was established in May 1991 by the European Foundation for the Improvement of Living and Working Conditions based in Dublin. The countries participating in the action research within the EC in Eurocounsel are Denmark, Germany, Italy, Ireland, Spain and the United Kingdom. In addition one EFTA country, Austria, is involved, its participation paid for by the Austrian government. EUROCOUNSEL has now reached the end of the second phase of its work and this is the synthesis report of all that has happened during Phase 2.

Background to Eurocounsel

The European Foundation for the Improvement of Living and Working Conditions undertook two programmes of work related to long-term unemployment during the 1980s. This work centred on the unemployed individual and the local context within which he or she has to deal with the many complex social and economic realities of unemployment. It also stressed the need to involve all those concerned in processes of structural change and to improve co-ordination of the various agencies operating at different levels. Towards the end of the 1980s when unemployment rates were in fact falling in many countries in Europe, the Foundation became concerned as to whether there was a lack of information, advice and counselling for the long-term unemployed and whether this might be influencing the apparent low take up of jobs by the long-term unemployed. It was considered that advice and counselling systems could help individuals to reach informed and realistic decisions about training and employment opportunities and facilitate the allocation of human resources. They could also perform an important reintegrative role in helping those who are disadvantaged to compete more equally for jobs and training. The Foundation identified that to date little attention had been focused on such roles.

The feasibility study

In 1989 a feasibility study was commissioned by the Foundation to investigate both whether the subject area of counselling and long-term unemployment was one which merited further attention, and to test whether the method of action research was an appropriate one. The results of the feasibility work were highlighted in two booklets, one for policy makers and one for practitioners. (Ref: 3 and 4)

The feasibility work took place in two local labour market areas: Storstrøms Amt a county in the south of Denmark and Inverclyde District, in the west of the central lowlands of

Scotland. The work involved mapping all the counselling services in these two areas and interviewing a range of counselling practitioners and policy makers. Two local consultations were held, one in each area to which participants from the other area as well as local practitioners were invited.

To avoid spending a disproportionate amount of time and effort in refining definitions, especially since it was recognised that there is ongoing debate as to precise meanings, the Eurocounsel team decided to adopt a working definition of "counselling" for the course of the study. This consisted of four main elements:

- **Information: the presentation of objective facts**
  For example: this is the law: these are your rights, obligations, options. For other information go to X or Y: for advice, counselling, guidance, go to Z or somewhere else. Or even, "I am now changing roles and moving from information-giving to counselling (or guidance)".

- **Guidance: how to use information**
  Having established the situation, options, possibilities, this is how you can set about using the information; this is what will/may happen if you choose such-and-such an option. Especially used in the light of:
  - the labour market situation;
  - the "facts" (educational attainment, psychological capacity, results of skill tests etc.). Here are the jobs/careers for which you are suitable, and there are the qualifications you have to gain and the ways in which you can gain them.

- **Advice: what I (or an agency) think you should do**
  In the light of the facts about you and the labour market and other relevant factors, this is what I would do if I were in your place and what I think you would be best advised to do. Advice can also be more "official", i.e. in your situation, this is what the authorities think you should do and they advise you to do it. This more "directive" approach is also somehow used in "guidance", i.e. not only is this how you can set about getting a job, but it is how we (the authorities) expect/insist you should act: and there are sanctions for not following our advice/guidance.

- **Counselling: a process of achieving informed and self-responsible understanding for a client on how to tackle their circumstances**
  The emphasis in counselling is/should be more on the process which results from the relationship between the counsellor and the client, an educational and/or social work activity. It can be undertaken by independent counsellors acting as professional consultants according to a professional ethos or code, or by persons, whether

professional counsellors or not, only with a defined system with presented objectives and limits. In such circumstances the possibilities of wholly "non-directive" counselling have to be limited and expanded according to the objective of the service or programme in which counselling is employed.

Counsellors need to know the information which is relevant, they should be able to guide and advise (either on their own initiative or only when asked), and if given the time and opportunity, assist clients to arrive at their own decisions and choices in the light of the information, guidance and advice available. The extent to which this is generally possible will depend on the extent to which legal, financial or social sanctions are operating.

The term "counselling" has been used throughout Eurocounsel to denote all of these meanings.

As a result of the feasibility work, an initial framework was designed to aid analysis of the results. This framework has remained useful in the first two phases of the programme. It involves four key areas:

-       an overview of **the systems in each country** so that the context in which counselling services are offered can be given; the systems include political, institutional and cultural elements as these all affect the services provided. In particular the approach to unemployment and labour market measures was examined;

-       issues relating to **access to counselling services**, including both physical access (geographical, buildings, outreach, etc) but also mental or psychological access such as the image of the service and users' perceptions of it; in short, all the aspects which make services accessible or not have been included in this area;

-       the **process of the counselling provision** itself; how is it delivered and what forms does it take? The findings during the feasibility stage and in Phase 1 were that the commonest form of counselling content provided was that of information giving;

-       the **outcomes of counselling** and how these are measured; the findings here were that outcomes were infrequently measured and where they were the measurements tended to be quantitative rather than qualitative.

The feasibility study concluded that the subject merited further attention and that the process of action research was a useful one, not least because the inputs of practitioners and policy makers alike had greatly contributed to its positive results. The Foundation decided therefore to launch a full programme to undertake work in a number of countries throughout Europe with the overall aim to improve counselling services for the unemployed and those at risk of becoming so, examining the role counselling can play in tackling long-term unemployment as part of an integrated package of labour market measures.

Phase 1 of Eurocounsel

During Phase 1 researchers were appointed in each of the participating countries and termed "local consultants". (See Appendix 1). The overall team was co-ordinated by Glenys Watt of Blake Stevenson Ltd a research and consultancy company specialising in economic and social development with a particular focus on the labour market. The Austrian government joined the programme during the course of Phase I.

In Phase 1 the local consultants undertook a mapping exercise of counselling services in one or two local labour market areas in their country. They set this in the context of the national systems, following the same analytical framework designed during the feasibility study described above. Each country held a consultation day/s to which practitioners and policy makers from the two local areas were invited. This was to allow for full discussion of the key issues affecting counselling provision related to their own situation.

The results of the first phase have been written up in a synthesis report entitled "Counselling and Long-term Unemployment". (Ref: 1) A short summary is also available in each of the Community's nine languages. (Ref: 2)

The Phase 1 report deepened understanding of counselling provision in the participating countries. In particular it identified three different functions which counselling may play, according to varying local labour market situations. Whilst these definitions are not totally free-standing and counselling services in practice can often range across more than one of them, they do provide useful indications of the flexibility which services require if they are to meet the needs of their users, as well as of their complexity:

- **solving or matching** the supply of labour to the demand for labour, is a function which is more commonly found in dynamic labour markets where the counselling service supports the user in finding employment and at the same time assists employers to fill their vacancies;

- **coping**, which includes both assisting the unemployed person to deal with the situation of unemployment but also to pro-actively find ways to create work and activity through job creation and local economic development, is particularly suited to areas where there is a low demand for labour and/or an over-supply of labour;

- **prevention** is a function of counselling services aimed at preventing long-term unemployment. It is commonly found where a public or private sector organisation knows that it is going to have to make people redundant and in situations where people are newly unemployed; its purpose is to provide counselling at an early stage rather than wait for someone to become long-term unemployed. This preventive function of counselling with its focus on early intervention is less commonly found but is seen more often in large industry restructurings such as coal, shipbuilding and steel.

The Phase I report produced a number of key findings which are summarised below.

A range of services and approaches is in existence within the labour market areas studied

The amount of counselling available and its level of sophistication varies from country to country. There are also variations in the approaches taken to the provision of counselling. Generally however, counselling is being regarded increasingly as having a pivotal role to play in the better functioning of the labour market as well as being an essential service for the individual.

Access, Process and Outcomes

Counselling services are seldom accessed for their own sake, but mostly as a consequence of a necessary contact with statutory agencies whose counselling is mostly related to their own area of responsibility such as the provision of benefits or education and training courses. There is a need to improve co-ordination and collaboration between the various providers and services so that the user is able to gain access to the most appropriate services for their needs.

Evidence of an intensive and extended customer-centred approach remains the exception. Services which focus on the preventive function are also rare. There are only a few examples of follow-on counselling, where the unemployed person who has found a job is given continuing counselling support.

Assessment of the outcomes of counselling is difficult partly because of the different elements within the counselling (information, advice, guidance, counselling) which might each have different outcomes, as well as the varying situations in which counselling is offered. There is little evidence of measurement of outcomes and what exists tends to focus only on quantitative measures.

The user as a customer

In general terms the first phase of Eurocounsel highlighted the need to focus more attention on the user as a customer, with all the attention to the customer's requirements and provision of a quality service which this entails.

Issues for the social partners

There is scope for employers and trade unions to become more involved in the future in the provision of counselling services. Employers can benefit from closer involvement with those involved in the provision of employment related counselling. Trade Unions' involvement has been limited due partly to the fact that their membership is largely composed of those who are in work. In situations of mass redundancies, however, they have a clear role in supporting and offering counselling services to their members.

Issues for practitioners

The main concerns identified by practitioners included:

- training and the need for professionalisation;

- difficulties in accessing up-to-date and practical information about the labour market;

- the problem of measuring outcomes;

- the importance of networking.

Issues for government policy makers

The key issues for government policy makers focused around the following areas:

- the need for decentralisation of services in order to become more responsive to the users' needs, balanced with the need to operate within national frameworks for policy measures;

- financial resources for counselling;

- the measurement and assessment of value for money.

A wider role for counselling?

The role which counselling can play in helping to make the labour market work more efficiently is being recognised, not just in the transition from unemployment to employment, but in the many other transitions which individuals face during the course of their working life.

The Phase I report concluded that it would be useful in Phase 2 to increase the transnational element of the programme so that the work of the first phase could be built on.

2 PHASE 2 OF EUROCOUNSEL

The report structure

The content and structure of this report is as follows:

- Chapter 2 outlines the work which has been undertaken during Phase 2 of the programme;

- Chapter 3 provides a brief summary of the overall context in each of the participating countries' and gives a cross-country analysis based on the local consultants' reports;

- Chapter 4 describes the process and outcomes of the collection and production of the portfolio of case studies and presents the key outcomes from the three transnational elements of this phase:

    - the seminar for senior government officials;

    - the pilot programme of study visits;

    - the Eurocounsel conference held in Dublin in May 1993.

- Chapter 5 presents the key findings from the whole of this second phase of Eurocounsel;

- Chapter 6 describes proposals for the next stage of Eurocounsel.

Phase 2 programme of work

Phase 2 of Eurocounsel has contained three main elements of work:

- feedback and dissemination of the Phase 1 findings and monitoring and support activities in the participating local labour market areas;

- research, collection, assessment, editing and publication of a portfolio of case studies of interesting/innovative experience;

- a transnational element, including a seminar for senior government officials, a pilot programme of study visits for practitioners, and the holding of a major international Eurocounsel conference to which participants from all the Member States as well as countries outside the European Community were invited.

The first of these elements is described in detail in this chapter while the second and third are outlined here and the results from them presented in Chapter 4.

Feedback and Dissemination

Feedback and dissemination of the work of Eurocounsel has taken place in a number of different ways. Within the seven countries the local consultants have given verbal and written feedback. This has involved meetings with those who were interviewed in the participating local labour market areas during the Phase 1 research, as well as in some cases such as Italy, meetings with people in areas which were not directly involved. Dissemination has involved the distribution of the summary of the Phase 1 report (which has been translated into all nine languages of the Community) together with each national report to a range of policy makers, social partners and practitioners. Examples of the way in which the local consultants have undertaken this work are given below as an indication of the extent to which the giving of feedback and the dissemination of information has been covered. The examples are not exhaustive of what has been achieved in each case, but serve as an illustration of the different approaches taken.

Austria	:	The Phase I reports were distributed to key decision-makers and in each of the two participating areas, Linz and Graz, full feedback meetings were held.
Denmark	:	The Danish local consultant has been involved in a range of European level meetings connected to other research work on guidance issues which he is engaged in. At these he has been able to present Eurocounsel. Notably, contacts have been developed with the EFTA countries.
Germany	:	The local consultants published a book of the results of the local consultation held in Phase I entitled "The individual counselling needs of the long-term unemployed in Eastern and Western Germany", which has been widely distributed.
Ireland	:	A range of meetings organised at national as well as local level to present Eurocounsel findings of Phase I, including meetings with the Irish Congress of Trade Unions, the Irish National Organisation of the Unemployed, the PESP central co-ordinating team and FAS, national manpower agency.

Italy : In one of the local labour market areas where the consultants are working, Trieste in the region of Friuli-Venezia-Giulia, the feedback on Phase I led to an invitation to the consultants to prepare a proposal to reform local labour policy, including structures for counselling. Discussions on the Phase I findings were held in many parts of Italy.

Spain : Preparation of a report (October 1992) to provide information on Eurocounsel Phase I and the plans for Phase 2, sent to all policy-makers and practitioners who had been involved in Phase I. Involvement with two radio programmes, one a series about the Andalusian economy which devoted a whole programme to Eurocounsel, the other on Radio America as part of a round table discussion.

United Kingdom : Direct feedback to the network of counselling and guidance practitioners formed in the participating local labour market area (Bradford).

At international level members of the Eurocounsel team have made links with other European organisations and programmes concerned with issues relating to counselling and long-term unemployment. These include CEDEFOP, the ILO, OECD, the European Commission's ERGO programme, and the Task Force on Human Resources. Within individual countries there have also been linkages, for example, with the Horizon Programme in Ireland and NOW in Spain. The findings and work of Eurocounsel have been presented as part of the work undertaken during the course of Phase 2 at the meeting for Senior Government Officials (January 1993) and at the meeting of the Advisory Committee and local consultants held in Seville (February 1993) to which participants from the two Spanish local labour market areas were invited as well as at the Eurocounsel conference in Dublin (May 1993). Eurocounsel has also been presented by the co-ordinators, Blake Stevenson Ltd, at a number of different international meetings including the following:

- presentation of Eurocounsel at a workshop during the UK's conference to mark its tenure of the EC Presidency entitled "The Future for Public Employment Services" (September 1992);

- design and facilitation of a one week seminar on occupational counselling for senior policy makers from the Czech and Slovak Republics which included an overview of Eurocounsel (Prague, January 1993), supported by the EC's Phare programme;

- conference speech at the Austrian national consultation two day event in Mürzuschlag (March 1993).

Monitoring and support

In each country the local consultants have remained in contact with the participating local labour market areas. They have been able to provide support and advice as appropriate. In some cases, such as that of Trieste in Italy, this support has been quite extensive in terms of designing concrete proposals for improvements to services and facilitating consensus to implement them. The local consultants' role has also involved monitoring of the national context and keeping informed about new developments in relation to the provision of counselling. As can be seen in the next chapter, this monitoring of the national context is an essential element as it is constantly changing and has direct, as well as indirect, results on the provision of counselling. The key issues emerging from this element of the work are presented in the next chapter.

Portfolio of case studies

As part of their work in Phase 2, each of the local consultants was asked to research and present three examples of interesting and innovative practice in counselling provision from their country. These have been compiled into a portfolio of case studies. (Ref: 7) A commentary on this case study portfolio is given in Chapter 4.

The transnational component

A key focus of Phase 2 has been to increase the transnational element of Eurocounsel. This has comprised four parts each of which is described briefly below and is examined in more depth in Chapter 4.

Pilot programme of study visits

A pilot programme of study visits for practitioners from the participating local labour market areas has been organised during Phase 2. The programme was co-ordinated by Blake Stevenson Ltd with the assistance of the local consultants. A total of 18 practitioners took part visiting 7 countries.

Seminar for senior government officials

A three day seminar for senior government officials from public employment services was held in January 1993 in Edinburgh. (Ref: 5) Twelve policy makers attended the meeting, coming from each of the participating countries except Spain and in addition there was representation from France, Sweden and the Netherlands. The meeting was facilitated by the Blake Stevenson team. The seminar was co-sponsored by the UK's Employment Service and the Foundation.

The Eurocounsel conference

A three day international conference was held in the conference centre of the Foundation in Dublin in May 1993 for around one hundred delegates from all the participating countries and in addition from Sweden, the USA, Finland, France, the Netherlands, the CSFR, Belgium, Greece and Portugal. (Ref: 6) The event was co-sponsored by the European Commission and by FAS, the Irish Training and Employment Agency.

Final comments

The work of Phase 2 has been successful in introducing a transnational element and has produced a wealth of results. As will be seen in the next chapters of this report, these results have served to deepen the work of Eurocounsel and to lead it in new directions which will require further research.

It is appropriate to thank all those who have worked so hard to achieve the successful outcomes of Phase 2, including the Advisory Committee, (see Appendix I) the co-sponsoring bodies, the research team, the host organisations for the study visits and not least all those within the participating countries who have given time and assistance in the programme.

3   THE COUNTRY REPORTS AND CROSS-COUNTRY ANALYSIS

This chapter examines each of the seven country reports produced by the researchers involved in Eurocounsel.

There is an enormous amount of detailed information and useful analysis in each of the local consultant's reports. The main focus in this chapter is to provide a summary overview of the context relating to counselling provision in each country and then to cross-reference the key themes emerging from the reports, commenting on similarities and contrasting differences.

The background context and policy developments within each of the participating countries

AUSTRIA

In Austria, the only non-EC country participating in the Eurocounsel research, there has been a deterioration in the labour market situation similar to that seen in the six EC participating countries. (Ref: 8)   In April 1993 unemployment was at 6.9% which is still comparatively low in relation to the average in the European Community (now 12.4%) but which is a steep increase in Austria which is used to unemployment rates below 5%. At the same time as the increase in the numbers of people who are unemployed, there is a decrease in the numbers of jobs available. There are therefore more people in need of counselling services.

The Austrian labour market administration is attempting to meet this increased need for counselling in four main ways:

-       through the establishment of a training institute providing courses for counsellors in the employment offices;

-       through increased efforts to place unemployed people in the primary labour market (including stricter control of benefits);

-       through use of non-profit counselling agencies which provide counselling related to the labour market on a contract basis for the labour market administration;

-    through an expansion of the Labour Foundation model as well as other active labour
     market measures.

The Federal Ministry of Labour and Social Affairs has made a renewed attempt in 1993 to
establish general conditions for the non-profit counselling agencies through the design of
Guidelines for the contracts between the provincial employment offices and the non-profit
counselling agencies. These guidelines emphasise the desire for a comparable method of
performance measurement in all counselling facilities and the need to target counselling
resources on those who are disadvantaged but for whom there is a high probability of
reintegration into the labour market. The relationship between the public employment
offices and the non-profit counselling agencies is one which has been widely discussed
during the course of 1993, and is central to an analysis of counselling provision in Austria.

DENMARK

During Phase 2 of Eurocounsel unemployment in Denmark has grown by approximately 3%
to a national average of 13.2%. (Ref: 9)   There has been a shift at national level, openly
expressed by politicians, away from full employment as the only goal for policy in this
area. This has led to a new approach involving "activation" strategies designed to prevent
people from becoming too passive in unemployment.

The activation strategy includes a widening of the concept of work and introduction of
alternatives to paid employment such as voluntary work, a relatively new concept in the
Danish social system. Counselling is seen as an important component of the activation
process. There are some interesting examples in the Danish report of self-help groups at
local level supporting each other in job creation and other forms of activation.

The main focus of Denmark's strategy to deal with the problem of unemployment however
is still on training and education, through various job offers and education offers which are
available to people who have been out of work for certain defined periods.

One recent development in this area is to support the need for upgrading skills within the
existing workforce, while at the same time allowing the unemployed to have a real work
experience. This is known as the job rotation scheme. The worker is able to take up to
nine months off work for training purposes and the unemployed person has the opportunity
to work again for a real wage. Counselling is required at several points in this process: for
the unemployed person, for the person who is taking study leave and for the employer.

Another key issue which emerged in the course of Phase 2 arose as a result of research on the job-offer and training offer schemes in which 22% of the unemployed claimed not to have received counselling from the unemployment insurance funds or from the employment service. This contrasts with the recognition at government level that there is possible duplication of counselling services between the municipalities, the unemployment insurance funds and the public employment service (AF) all of which offer counselling for different but overlapping groups.

To sum up, two main threads dominate the Danish situation: that of the need to find alternatives to formal employment in the first labour market, and secondly the view of counselling as part of a learning process. The Danish system leans heavily towards the provision of learning and training, and counselling services are readily available within this provision .

GERMANY

There are two major differences in the German situation as described by the German local consultants in their report for this second phase, (Ref: 10) compared with that of the first phase of Eurocounsel:

-    the hopes that the economic problems of reunification were transitional and could be overcome fairly quickly are fading, and long-term unemployment is now part of the context in eastern Germany;

-    Germany has been hit by the worldwide recession and this, together with the problems of reunification, has caused rapidly rising unemployment in the west and east. Unemployment has risen by 50% in the west and in the east the high levels of unemployment have persisted.

The costs of dealing with these economic problems have resulted in attempts to make savings elsewhere in government public expenditure. In the west, the employment services are charged with enforcing stricter controls on those claiming benefits to reduce any abuse of the system and thus enable savings to be made. There is a possibility that if these controls do not produce the required savings that benefits themselves will be reduced. Other cost savings have seen a reduction in the kinds of counselling services available so that less preventive work can be done. There has also been a reduction in the employment services' contacts with employers, thus lessening the scope for collaboration at this level. Those in employment are now excluded from employment counselling.

The west German counselling services are also experiencing a change in the kinds of client with whom they deal. Previously those who were unemployed were either perceived to have, or in reality did have, some form of psychological or social problems as the labour market was so buoyant. Now however, there is an increase in the number of unemployed who in times of low unemployment would have required minimal assistance to re-enter the labour market and who have different needs in relation to counselling, which in turn requires adaptation to existing services. This need to adapt services comes at a time of increased pressure on resources as described above.

In the east, in Thüringen, which is the local labour market area participating in Eurocounsel, counselling services are provided primarily by a voluntary sector initiative, ALI (Arbeitsloseninitiative Thüringen), which has employed most of its counsellors through 2 year temporary job contracts under the ABM scheme. These job contracts all ended in 1992 and led to a period of crisis. ALI has had to concentrate its efforts on seeking financial support and the survival of its work in this area. This had led to waste in terms of the training and experience which these counsellors, whose contracts have been terminated, received.

The overall sense of the situation for counselling services in Germany portrayed in this report is one of pessimism. The strength of the economic crisis it appears has come as something of a surprise in the western part of the country and in the eastern part, what was hoped to be a transitional problem, is now seen as one which is more deep-seated.

IRELAND

The unemployment situation in Ireland has continued in its severity. (Ref: 11)   Ireland has the second highest rate of unemployment in the European Community at 18.6%. Within this there are a particularly large number of young unemployed people.

The final report of Phase I in Ireland identified a number of key areas for the development of provision in relation to counselling, guidance, advice and information services to the unemployed. These included:

-       the importance of accurately identifying the needs of the long-term unemployed to include the range of employment, welfare and personal needs;

-        the need to develop provision with an outreach dimension;

-        the need for improved systems of referral between providers, which might partly be achieved through more networking as well as through formal documentation of the services provided;

-        greater linking of counselling within other labour market measures; and

-        issues relating to the training of counselling practitioners.

During Phase 2 of Eurocounsel there have been significant developments in the national context and in specific areas relating to the above. At national level the main issue identified by the local consultants is the "growing recognition of the importance of guidance and counselling for the long-term unemployed", although it is suggested that to some extent this recognition has led mainly to informal integration within the existing institutional framework.

A second key development in Ireland is the establishment of twelve local area based companies under the government funded Programme for Economic and Social Progress. These PESP companies, which are partnership bodies formed from the statutory and voluntary sectors, businesses and trade unions, are attempting among other things to address the over-centralisation of services in Ireland by developing strategies and programmes which meet local needs.

ITALY

The situation in Italy in the first phase of the Eurocounsel programme appeared very different to that in the other participating countries in that although there were generally centralised employment policies these did not seem to recognise the provision of counselling as an important measure in the Italian context. The main approach was one of incentives to employers to maintain their work-force and of social welfare for those who became unemployed. This was particularly true in the north of the country as it experienced a period of economic growth between 1984-1991. As the Italian report points out, (Ref: 12) in this part of the country unemployment was almost seen as a self-chosen state.

However as in other parts of Europe, 1992 -1993 has brought a period of economic crisis to most parts of Italy and this has been compounded in the Italian situation by political and institutional crises. It is, as the Italian consultant puts it, a situation of fundamental crisis out of which new opportunities may arise. There is a search at present for new models at local and regional levels, whose success will depend partly on developments at national level. It appears that there is a leaning towards new policies which will:

-       allow for decentralisation, so that Regions will have responsibility for their employment policies;

-       increased intervention towards specific target groups;

-       measures to establish individual projects.

The economic crisis is compounded by the problems of the public finances. As the local consultants write:

> "... the Italian national debt is at the moment virtually out of control, so in addition to policies to drag it back, it is also necessary to plan a change from a model of intervention based exclusively on subsidies and incentives, to less expensive and more effective modes" (Geroldi and Maiello. Ref: 12, p.3)

The key issues for the Italian situation in relation to the provision of counselling are summed up at the end of the report as being twofold:

-       that for counselling services in Italy to improve radically will require significant change, both politically and culturally;

-       that access to services is not just a question of efficiency but is more fundamentally one of democracy.

There is a strong sense in reading the Italian report that the opportunities are now emerging in which Italy could see fairly rapid improvements in the provision of counselling services and a sense that if these opportunities are not seized that the political situation will have moved away from greater democracy.

SPAIN

During Phase I of Eurocounsel in Spain the following key needs were identified at the National Consultation (which was held in Seville in March 1992):

- the need to co-ordinate counselling services operating within the same area;

- the need to find appropriate methods to improve local labour market information and knowledge;

- the need to develop counselling techniques appropriate to the specific needs of the users;

- the need to train municipal practitioners involved in the provision of counselling.

At the same time it was recognised that the local labour market situation in the two participating local labour market areas differed. In the area of Campiña de Sevilla in Andalusia in the south the supply of labour outstrips the demand so that counselling linked to employment creation strategies is required whereas in Badalona opportunities in the first labour market are greater.

At national level the period of Phase 2 of Eurocounsel has seen a worsening economic situation. (Ref: 13) Spain now has the highest unemployment rate in the EC (at 21%). This in turn has led to budget cutbacks in the various administrations concerned with provision for the unemployed. The government during this period has pursued a policy of reforming the labour market by making the regulation of the labour market less rigid. This has included controversial actions such as the reduction of the cost of dismissal for employers and the bureaucracy associated with it.

Law 22/1992, which was passed in July 1992 set out the government's three main areas of action in relation to employment policy. These are:

- a plan to improve the management of unemployment benefits, which will involve measures to ensure that those in receipt of benefit are actively seeking work and are not undertaking undeclared work while still receiving benefits;

- a public programme to promote recruitment under permanent contracts of employment, which will emphasise incentives and subsidies for the creation of new jobs;

-       reform of the system providing protection against unemployment.

The second key issue at national level in Spain has been the proposed reforms of the Instituto Nacional de Empleo (INEM). The changes are not yet finally agreed but may include the transfer of administration of unemployment benefits from INEM to the social security authorities. There have also been ongoing discussions in the media about the possibility of privatising INEM. These expected changes have led to a great deal of uncertainty for those working in INEM which in turn has had some effect on the work of Phase 2 of Eurocounsel at local level, where proposed actions had to be amended. Finally, the report highlighted the fact that with a general election to be held in June 1993, many expected legislative changes were necessarily on hold causing a certain paralysis in the country.

UNITED KINGDOM

Unemployment in the UK has remained high during Phase 2 but the recession had already begun to hit hard during the first phase of Eurocounsel and so there is less sense here than in some of the other countries that there has been a dramatic change. The average national level of unemployment is now around 11%. (Ref: 14)

A package of new employment measures has been introduced by the government in March 1993, which it is estimated will provide around 100,000 more opportunities to help unemployed people. These include a new community based scheme "Community Action"; a new scheme, "Learning for Work", which will allow people to take full-time vocational education and training courses and retain an allowance equivalent to their benefit; (which is a new development in the UK as those who are in receipt of unemployment benefit until now have only been able to take part-time courses in order not to disturb their availability for work requirement); "Workstart Pilots", four in number, which are intended to test different approaches to giving employers incentives to provide opportunities for unemployed people. Two other elements of the package consist of further assistance to unemployed individuals to start up their own businesses and assistance to the locally-based Training and Enterprise Councils to stimulate them to develop innovative ways to tackle unemployment.

Counselling will be an important element in all of these. In general terms, there has been an increase in awareness at national level of the important role counselling has to play in assisting the long-term unemployed. This is illustrated by the introduction in April in 1993 by the public Employment Service of the Jobplan Workshops which involves an intensive one week's counselling for groups of up to twelve long-term unemployed participants at a time. The Jobplan Workshops (and their option for professional unemployed people, the Job Review Workshops) are undertaken by independent providers, mostly within the private sector, acting as sub-contractors to the Employment Service. This independence is perceived by participants as important as it lessens the perception of control or compulsion which is sometimes associated with provision by the Employment Services themselves.

Another interesting development promoted by the area based Training and Enterprise Councils (in England and Wales) and the Local Enterprise Companies (in Scotland) is that of learning, career development and counselling shops. There are now around twenty-five such "shops" throughout the UK, each one slightly different in character according to the local situation in which it finds itself. These are innovative developments as they attempt not to stigmatise counselling services as being only for the unemployed but make them available to the whole adult population. They address the important issue that unemployment is a possibility for most people at some time in their working lives and that it is important to take responsibility for your own career progress and seek out opportunities for new learning and training. They are set in the context in the UK of the need to increase the skill base available within the whole labour force.

In Bradford, the local labour market area participating in Eurocounsel, as in some other parts of the UK, a Guidance Voucher system has been introduced which aims to give more choice to the unemployed user of counselling services and at the same time attempts to foster a market of counselling services from which to choose. There is a rapid growth in private sector services which offer counselling not only to those who are already unemployed but also to those who are about to be made redundant.

CROSS-COUNTRY ANALYSIS

The next section of this chapter analyses some of the key points emerging from the country reports and draws out interesting similarities and differences. For ease of reference the main headings from the initial analytical framework are used, namely systems, access, process and outcomes.

NATIONAL CONTEXT AND SYSTEMS

Rising unemployment

All the reports make mention of the growth in unemployment and the concern which this is raising. In some countries the increase in unemployment is regarded as more dramatic than others. For example in Germany there appears to have been some surprise that the situation with regard to unemployment is so bad, while in the UK there is more of a sense that the recession has existed for some time with ever-increasing unemployment. A table of current national unemployment figures is given below. It shows the severity of the situation particularly in Spain and Ireland. In several countries, there is open discussion about the unlikelihood of full employment returning. Only in a few areas in the north of Italy is the situation different and even there, there are signs that unemployment is now on the increase. (Although there is one notable exception in the local labour market areas which have participated in Eurocounsel that of Trento, Italy, where unemployment has fallen).

Clearly the situation is causing major concern and unemployment is now back at the top of the priority list on the European agenda. Latest unemployment figures show that the unemployment rate in the European Community has been rising for the last seventeen months, the last decrease having been recorded in December 1991. The implications for counselling services in the light of this situation are many and include:

-        the obvious rise in demand for services among those who are unemployed;

-        the heightened difficulties for practitioners in helping the user find positive outcomes, especially in areas of low demand for labour;

-        pressure on resources which may be required to meet unemployment benefit payments.

Table 1

UNEMPLOYMENT FIGURES

Unemployment Rates Seasonally Adjusted: May 1992 and 1993 (%)

Total: Male and Female

	EUR 12	DK	D	ESP	IRL	IT	UK	*AUS
May 1992	9.4	9.5	4.4	17.6	17.5	10.1	10.6	5.2
May 1993	10.5	10.6	5.5	21.0	18.6	10.7	11.3	6.2

Source: EUROSTAT

*   Austrian figure supplied by Federal Ministry of Labour and Social Affairs "Labour Market Data, 1993".

Stricter controls on benefits

Several of the reports (Austria, Germany, Spain and UK) make specific mention of the fact that stricter controls are being introduced to ensure that only those who are eligible receive unemployment benefit. In Germany there is discussion about the possibility of cutting benefits in order to make savings in the budget.

Compulsory counselling and benefits

Related to the issue of stricter controls on benefits is the question of whether it is useful or unhelpful to link counselling services to the provision of benefits. In Spain it is interesting to note that it is proposed that the responsibility for benefits be moved from INEM, the national employment agency, to the social security authorities. The element of compulsion is still retained at present (Law 22/1992) where unemployed people are obliged to undertake occupational guidance or training where so required if they wish to retain their right to remain registered as a job-seeker or continue receiving financial benefits. In other countries, for example in the UK, counselling services for the long-term unemployed are linked to continuance of benefit. The argument for a compulsory system is that it catches those who have need of counselling assistance who might otherwise not seek it out for themselves. Those against this compulsory linking perceive it as contrary to adopting a client-centred approach because the needs of the agency offering the service are to the forefront.

Limited resources

The economic crisis brought about by the recession is causing real difficulties in terms of resources. Most of the reports make reference to the problem and its effects on the provision of counselling services. It appears to be most severe in Germany where the numbers of counselling practitioners are actually being reduced and further budgetary savings are being sought. The only report where the emphasis is rather different is the Italian one where the question of whether the provision of counselling services is increased or not, appears to be related to cultural and political change as much as to the availability of resources. In Italy there has been a tendency to make use of welfarism alone to deal with unemployment and resources have tended to be concentrated in this area.

Importance of counselling at national level

There are contrasts in the levels of importance ascribed to counselling at national level within the seven participating countries. In some countries such as Ireland and the UK there appears to have been an increase in the importance given to counselling at national level, in particular for the long-term unemployed. The introduction of the Jobplan Workshops in the UK and of counselling within the Community Employment Development Programme in Ireland highlight this. In others countries, such as Denmark and Austria, the sense of counselling as important has continued to be firmly embedded. However in Italy and Spain it appears there is not the same importance attached to counselling at *national* level although there are indications that at regional and local levels this can vary widely. In both countries there are examples at local and regional levels of developments in the provision of counselling. In Germany the pressure on resources means that counselling services are under threat as politicians try to prioritise how to spend resources in a difficult situation.

Decentralisation

Criticisms were made in some of the Phase I country reports of the over-centralisation of service provision. In Phase 2 there is a political trend towards decentralisation in all of the countries examined and this has particular implications for the provision of counselling services. In some instances, such as the locally based companies set up under the Programme for Economic and Social Progress in Ireland, the decentralisation process is allowing for closer targeting of services to meet people's needs. However local provision can also have its drawbacks. In Spain the municipalities, which are taking more responsibility for service provision, are hindered by constraints on resources. The decentralisation process may lead to increased diversification of the counselling services available. For example, in Denmark in the future, central authorities will issue guidelines for activation measures and will allocate funding, which the regional authorities will be able to decide how to spend, within given broad criteria. In Spain there have been significant moves towards decentralisation in the areas of the management of vocational training and occupational education. Even in Italy where traditionally there has been high centralisation of employment policies there are increasing expressions of the need to transfer legislative powers to the Regions in matters concerning employment.

Role of the Social Partners

There is evidence in the country reports to suggest that the role of employers is becoming more pronounced in relation to counselling provision than was the case in Phase I. For example, in Austria in the Linz region, it is noted that there is a desire for the expansion and development of the relations between counselling agencies (both public and non-profit) and companies. As new approaches to making the labour market more flexible are developed in order to allow those who are unemployed opportunities for work experience, such as the job rotation scheme in Denmark and similar schemes in Spain, the need for counselling to assist in making such schemes operate effectively becomes apparent. Not only the unemployed but also employers (and in situations involving rotation, existing employees) will require assistance.

In two of the national reports, those of Italy and Spain, the role of subsidies to employers to encourage them to take on the unemployed is raised. The Italian one suggests that the provision of such subsidies hinders the further development of counselling services: the argument is that it is easier in some situations to subsidise employers in order to defer making someone redundant.

The situation with regard to the trade unions is less clear. There is evidence that some trade unions are becoming more involved in training their own officials to be able to offer counselling (e.g. in Denmark) and unions have played a key role in situations of mass lay-offs in ensuring that a redundancy counselling service is offered (for example in Austria's Labour Foundations).

It is true however that the chief concern of the unions is with their members who are still in work. It was interesting to note that at the Eurocounsel conference in May 1993 in Dublin, the working group composed of union representatives suggested that unemployed workers would be greatly assisted by having more formal organisations and in particular by having unions for the unemployed. The question of the role of the trade unions in relation to the unemployed has been a continuing and complex challenge for the unions for a number of years and with unemployment in the EC now at 17 million and likely to increase, is an issue with which trade unions are likely to continue to struggle.

The role of partnerships

The social partners, again most frequently the private sector employers, are found in partnerships which have come together to provide counselling. The Austrian Arbeitsstiftungen (Labour Foundations) are an excellent example of such co-operation involving as they do the local authorities, the private sector company, employees themselves and the trade unions. Other examples are found in Ireland (the companies established under the Programme for Economic and Social Progress are partnership based) and in Spain INEM-Barcelona is working in collaboration with bodies which have concrete projects, such as the local authorities. Another example in Spain is the autonomous government of Catalonia which has recently introduced counselling practices that draw on private enterprises. However, it is true also that at local level partnerships and co-operative working are not always possible as agencies may wish to "claim success for themselves rather than enter into collaborative activities." (Spanish report. Ref: 13, p.51).

ISSUES RELATING TO ACCESS

Establishing/developing counselling services

A key issue of access to services is that the services should exist in the first place! The Italian report rightly highlights this point, by broadening the stated aims of Eurocounsel to include not just improvements to services but also the need to "contribute to their establishment if they do not already exist". (Ref: 12, p.98) There is evidence in the Italian and Spanish reports that new services are being established where previously none existed. For example, the Italian consultants were asked, partly as a result of their presentations on the findings of Phase I, to prepare a proposal for reform of labour policies (including the provision of counselling) in the region of Friuli-Venezia-Giuli, where Trieste is situated. This is an area which until now has had no explicit form of guidance or counselling for adults, employed or unemployed, and nowhere for job seekers to turn for specific support. Clearly access here is primarily about having services established.

The importance of outreach

The importance of developing better outreach services in both rural and urban areas was highlighted in the Phase I report. There is evidence that in Phase 2 in some of the most rural areas, this issue is being addressed. For example, in north Mayo in Ireland, provision is via a constantly travelling service which can adopt a holistic approach to the needs of those whom it serves. In Austria, in the region of Graz, there are attempts to establish a mobile counselling service in rural areas. In Italy too, in the autonomous province of Trento, the Labour Office has specialist workers operating in each of the 11 local areas within the Province. These specialists network with local units of the health and social welfare services and are able to assist those with more serious problems directly rather than waiting for them to come to one of the Office's two outlets in the Province. However, the Labour Office recognises the need for further improvements with regard to access and is moving towards a decentralisation of its services by opening up more outlets, where possible through existing structures.

Ensuring the user knows what the service has to offer

In terms of mental or psychological access to services, the Danish report highlights the development of "user maps" round the service i.e. "what can I as a user expect to get if I come to this service?" This approach is also developing in the UK where it fits in with the general move towards treating the client or user as a customer with certain rights.

Continuing diversity of services: growth in self-help and peer group counselling

The diversity of counselling services and the range of organisations offering them which was noted in the Phase 1 report, continues. Indeed in some countries it appears that the range of services available is growing rather than diminishing as limitations on resources restrict public sector provision and the urgency to tackle rising unemployment stimulates further action by non-government agencies. For example, in Spain, there is growth in the provision of counselling services via the not-for-profit sector. In Denmark there is a growing emphasis on self-help and peer group counselling. Similar examples are found in eastern Germany, Ireland, and Spain, and the Austrian report comments that counselling agencies there are keen to find ways to support self-help initiatives.

This diversity of service provision can have benefits for the unemployed person in terms of access but can also lead to confusion. The formalisation of local networks to link all the services together is one way to reduce such confusion and at least ensure that the services know each other. In Denmark the Regional Committees for Counselling are one such example and often less formalised similar networks are found in other countries too, particularly those with a longer tradition of counselling.

ISSUES RELATING TO THE PROVISION AND PROCESS OF COUNSELLING

The need for up to date and accurate information

The need for up to date and accurate information, about the local labour market and about training and learning opportunities has been well documented during the first phase of Eurocounsel. This need has still to be met and could provide one of the practical ways in which counselling services are improved. Proposals to address this issue and that of closer co-ordination by developing a local overall plan for co-ordination of counselling provision in the two areas involved in Eurocounsel in Spain were put forward by the Spanish local consultants but due to the re-organisation of the institutional structures in that country they were not able to be pursued further.

The role of new technology

There is surprisingly little mention made in the reports of the role of new technology in the provision of counselling although it was mentioned as important throughout the meetings held during Phase 2 of Eurocounsel. This may be partly due to oversight as computers and software packages are now widely available and used to assist in the initial stages of assessment, as well as in the management of information, in particular in northern countries. However, it is the Italian report which gives the strongest comments on this subject, referring to work in the autonomous province of Trento:

> "... the opinion which we have encountered is that an intelligent use of computers is now indispensable for managing guidance and counselling programmes ..." (Ref: 12, p.19)

Identification of needs

Several of the country reports raise the issue of involving the unemployed in the identification of their own needs in relation to counselling and the kinds of services they wish to have. This is particularly apparent in the Irish and German contexts. There is a need to examine more fully the examples of where unemployed people have been given an opportunity to have a direct influence on the kinds of services offered to them in order to provide examples of how this can be done effectively. This is one of the areas proposed for future research in the Austrian report.

A holistic approach to meeting needs?

As has been stated in many of the Foundation's own reports on long-term unemployment as well as in the European Commission's ERGO programme, the needs of the long-term unemployed are not homogeneous. (Ref: 24) Each individual is unique and will require different services from those who are providing counselling. One of the issues for consideration is whether services should try to meet all the needs of the individual, or at least be able to refer them to the appropriate services. For example, for many who have been out of work for a long time, financial matters and debt are the most pressing issue which they have to face. To insist on providing counselling for job/training/activity opportunities may be insensitive not to mention difficult if the person is anxious about their immediate financial situation. The Irish situation, as described in north Mayo, appears to try to meet all expressed needs from the outreach service. In the UK, some of those who are charged with running the Jobplan Workshops for the long-term unemployed are bringing in debt counsellors on their own initiative in order to meet expressed needs. In Austria however, in the region of Graz, the local consultant notes that there appears to be a separation into two counselling systems, one that claims to be exclusively labour market oriented and another that claims to be holistic/psycho-social. Proposals put forward by a team of Italian and Spanish practitioners during the Eurocounsel conference was for multi-disciplinary teams which would accept that there are a range of needs to be met which cannot be found in one single practitioner and that such a team would have more chance of meeting these needs. This issue will be referred to again later in the report.

Issues of where to target resources

As financial resources diminish, the political and economic question of who to target in terms of services arises. Some differing approaches are apparent from the national reports for Eurocounsel Phase 2. In Ireland, where the levels of the long-term unemployed are high, the local consultants argue that the needs of the long-term unemployed must be highlighted as otherwise they will become more and more marginalised or even forgotten. They quote from research in Ireland which has demonstrated that of all resources spent on the unemployed only 10% are targeted towards the long-term unemployed. In the northern wealthier parts of Italy on the other hand, the numbers of long-term unemployed are much lower and until recently these have been regarded as people who were unemployed because of specific problems. It was therefore thought that counselling assistance might be better targeted at the more recently unemployed. In Germany there is a sense that the necessity of helping the long-term unemployed is curtailing the services available for others. In the UK and Austria there are unofficial discussions as to whether to stop offering services after a certain time period (for example two- three years) and simply accept that some people will remain unemployed in order to allow all resources to be concentrated on those whom it is thought will be more easily reintegrated. In the Spanish report the problems of helping those most disadvantaged within the group of the unemployed is raised, especially the unskilled, people with disabilities, ex-offenders and gypsies. This important debate is discussed further in Chapter 5 of this report.

Counselling for the employed as well as the unemployed?

At the end of the Phase I report the question was raised as to whether counselling services should be made more widely available, to assist people in all the transitions relating to employment which they face as adults (moving to a new job; redundancy; preparing for retirement, etc). It is interesting to note that there are a few examples of this wider availability of services emerging from the reports. In the UK, the career development and learning shops offer a counselling and advice service to all adults. In Trento, one of Italy's autonomous provinces, the approach now emerging in the Labour Office involves the provision of information, guidance and counselling services for all people in the labour market. However this question is a difficult one at a time of diminishing resources and in some countries, e.g. Germany, counselling through the public employment service is no longer available for those in employment.

Targeted provision

In the Phase 1 report for Eurocounsel it was suggested that there was not enough targeted provision by counselling services in dealing with the unemployed. The extent to which targeting is found is not known precisely but a number of examples have appeared in the national reports including examples of services targeted at women (Germany, Austria and the UK), provision for minority ethnic communities (UK) and immigrants (Italy). The Spanish consultants suggest that one of the areas for future research in Spain might be to undertake a review of the counselling needs of immigrants. In Austria the establishment of the non-profit intermediary counselling services (see next paragraph) was to allow for this targeted approach to be developed. The aim there was to provide help for those who are most disadvantaged.

Counselling provision through intermediaries

There is evidence from the reports that public employment services in some countries are making greater use of intermediary organisations to undertake the provision of counselling on their behalf in a direct way through contracting with independent private, non-profit or voluntary sector agencies. This is a different model to that of the more traditional funding from central government for voluntary and non-profit organisations for activities which include counselling which has been common in some countries. In Austria the Labour Office contracts with non-profit agencies to work in particular with disadvantaged groups. In the UK more counselling provision is being sub-contracted to private and voluntary sector organisations. One of the issues which arises in working through intermediaries (as it does also in provision by any organisation) is that of quality and performance measurement. In some ways indeed it may be easier to set standards for measurement which sub-contractors have to meet, than monitoring performance internally. The Austrian Labour Office has drawn up criteria for performance measurement which it is currently discussing with its existing sub-contractors.

The use of personal action planning

In several countries the process of Personal Action Planning is increasingly used (Germany, UK and Spain). The Job Notebook case study (in Spain) is one example of such an approach. The purpose of such action planning is to provide the user with a written plan of the actions they will take next to achieve their longer term goals. It is one tangible outcome of a counselling process.

Preventive counselling

In some countries the preventive function which counselling can play is well developed. The Austrian Arbeitsstiftungen (Labour Foundations) provide a good example of what can be achieved. However in some countries such as Italy, the preventive role of counselling is still rare.

Counselling as a lubricant for other labour market measures

Counselling can be regarded as a lubricant which helps to make other active labour market measures more effective. For example, the job rotation scheme in Denmark benefits from counselling inputs with all the players involved. In Italy, in the Province of Trento, counselling is moving towards being the central service offered by the Labour Office, acting as a reference point for the activities of other programmes. In Linz, in Austria, the point is made that there needs to be an expansion of active employment measures to complement the employment office's counselling and information services.

Counselling linked to self-employment and new job creation

The issue of what kinds of counselling services should be offered in areas where there is low demand for labour has been further emphasised in the Phase 2 reports, in particular for the more remote rural areas of Ireland and Denmark, the southern parts of Italy and Spain, and eastern Germany. Unemployment is so intense in these areas, and the likelihood of jobs in the traditional labour market so limited, that this has to be a key concern. In all of these countries there is a growing demand for counselling services linked to self-employment and new job creation as well as for wider activities, as proposed in the Danish activation strategy. There have been several proposals in the country reports that this should be an area for future research.

A framework for counselling services in different labour market situations

The role of the social partners in the provision of counselling services depends to some extent on the economic and political situation in an area. The Italian report highlights this point and provides a framework which analyses the potential for the development of counselling services according to different local labour market situations. The model is a useful one, particularly with regard to the Italian context where services are not yet widely available. The framework identifies three general kinds of labour market:

- areas of poor development and mass unemployment (such as southern parts of Italy);

- areas which are declining particularly where there has been heavy reliance on one sector/industry;

- areas where there is only frictional unemployment (as in many parts of the north).

Alongside these labour market situations the Italian local consultants have diagnosed three main ways in which problems can be resolved:

- through co-operation;

-    through conflict (i.e. protest leads to resolution);

-    through manipulation, where the individual/group do not actually co-operate but nor do they rise in conflict because they are bought off in some way (for example, through welfare assistance or wage subsidies so that unemployment is deferred).

As the Italian report states this third form is not a midway point between conflict and co-operation but instead is one "characterised by the erosion of the logic of consensus " (Ref: 12, p.78).

"Top-down versus bottom-up"

Linked to this problem of what kinds of services to offer in labour markets where there is low demand for labour is an emerging debate within the national reports as to whether "top-down" counselling services, as are generally provided by public employment services, are "better" or whether "bottom-up" which develop at local level, often on the initiative of the unemployed themselves or as part of a local development process, are to be preferred. In our opinion, the answer to this question is neither. The whole range of services are required and as stated earlier one major key to improved services is to have good co-ordination between them.

The European Dimension of counselling

It is rather surprising that only two of the reports, the Danish and Spanish, make specific reference to the European dimension of counselling. This may be in part that the focus for most unemployed people, and therefore of counselling services, is on their own local area and not on moving to other areas of Europe. It may also reflect the fact that EURES, the European Commission's programme to facilitate the operation of the European labour market, and the Euro-counsellors trained to undertake its promotion in each country, are established only fairly recently (although prior to the creation of the Single Market, the European programme SEDOC provided labour market information to link the separate labour markets). It is also true to say that some of the local consultants are more connected to other European programmes than others. It is certainly evident that the importance of counselling and guidance is recognised at European level and there are a whole range of different angles being taken in work connected to this area by different European organisations (cf. the Eurocounsel conference description, Chapter 4).

OUTCOMES

Outcomes relating to counselling provision

All the national reports mention the importance of measuring outcomes and several have suggested that this is an area which requires further work in the future. Some of the local consultants have offered definitions of what the outcomes of counselling should be/are. For example, the Danish report quotes from a reference (Ref: 15) an analysis of the various potential learning outcomes of counselling. These are summarised as being concerned with:

- self-awareness;

- opportunity awareness;

- decision-taking skills;

- coping with change skills.

One of the important points made is that there is an underlying sense in Denmark that narrow technical skills must be linked with broader life skills "in order to accomplish individual employment success and fulfilment". The perception is that counselling helps with this broader approach.

The Irish report also defines the outcomes of counselling, within the framework of seeing it as a broadly focused intervention. The definition given has four main elements:

- direct employment outcomes (including self-employment or other income generating activities);

- entry into labour market re-integration schemes and programmes;

- outcomes in the area of combating social exclusion, seen as involvement in community or voluntary activity;

- personal development outcomes, which are seen as relating to the enhanced capacity of the long-term unemployed to understand the processes causing unemployment and to cope more effectively with the consequences of this.

It is possible to link these two sets of definitions together, to form two main strands of outcomes as shown below.

Table 2

OUTCOMES OF COUNSELLING

OPPORTUNITY AWARENESS LEADING TO SPECIFIC ACTION	PERSONAL DEVELOPMENT
* employment vacancies	* self-awareness
* employment creation	* awareness of reasons for unemployment
* voluntary work	* decision-taking skills
* community work	
* labour market programmes	* coping with change skills
* learning and training	

In terms of non-directive counselling, the aim is to see personal development at the core of opportunity awareness. There are other ways in which the outcomes can be defined. The starting point for agencies in examining how best to measure outcomes will be to have a clear and realistic idea of what they expect such outcomes to be. However, the needs of the user may lead to different emphases in terms of preferred outcomes. Recognising that these two sets of outcomes may not be exactly the same, given the objectives to which some agencies have to work, is important in terms of measurement and evaluation. At the same time the desired/possible outcomes will vary according to the labour market situation and will relate back to the different functions of counselling identified in Phase I - solving, coping and preventing. This issue of outcomes will be commented on again later in the report, in Chapter 5.

In terms of actual measurement of services, several of the reports offer commentaries as to the difficulties faced and issues involved. The German report describes how difficult it is to assess outcomes in the current unstable conditions, as training plans or even prospective employment may become unavailable at short notice. This can have a negative impact both on users and practitioners. The Spanish report emphasises the need to include both quantitative and qualitative criteria for measurements. The Irish report examines this whole issue of both quantitative and qualitative measurement in some detail (Duggan and Ronayne, 1993. (Ref: 11, pp 47-50). The consultants argue that even for quantitative measurement that basic data is unavailable, for example as to flows on and off the Live Register, making it difficult to contrast a group who have received counselling against a group who have not. Tracking of users, over a period of time, will be important. Where an outcome appears on immediate examination to be positive, for example securing a job, this needs to be checked as the type of employment, level of wages and likely stability over the longer term will all form part of the assessment as to how positive in fact the outcomes have been.

For qualitative measurement, the importance of assessing outcomes such as psychological well-being is identified. However, drawing too great a distinction between personal development outcomes and labour market ones may not be helpful. (cf. ERGO, Final Report, 1992). The timeframe for measuring outcomes which are qualitative in nature is again stressed. The Irish consultants also link qualitative assessment more directly to its impact on social exclusion rather than the more quantitative labour market inclusion.

The economic value of counselling

Linked to the measurement of results from counselling services is the need to undertake further work in assessing the economic value of counselling services. This was referred to in the synthesis Final Report for Phase I, and emerges as an issue in several of the reports. As the Danish report states: "In a number of respects, counselling is part of an overall attempt to create economic growth or, at least, stability". (Plant, 1993, P.68). There is growing recognition that it is, as the Danish local consultant writes, a "market-economic facilitator". But at the same time there is increasing emphasis on public acceptability. Some work has already been undertaken in this area within different EC countries. There are obvious difficulties associated with finding appropriate methodology, many linked to the issues discussed under measurement. Further work in this area is required.

Outcomes relating to the Eurocounsel programme in participating countries

Eurocounsel is an action research programme and this means that there have been a number of actions stimulated as well as direct research outcomes. With action research it is not always possible to predict what the outcomes will be (cf. Final Report Phase I, 1992). The local consultants' reports for Phase 2 illustrate this point and some examples from them are given below. Some of the outcomes will of course never be known as there is a sense of a ripple effect in action research, with one action leading to another and not always traceable back to the source.

Examples from the different reports include the following:

- in Austria, the participation in Eurocounsel has stimulated interest more generally in European programmes, in particular those which relate to labour market policy, and is seen to be an important step in bringing European experience closer to Austria as well as spreading Austrian know-how to EC countries;

- the Danish report cites an interesting example, where because attention had been focused on a project as a potential case-study example, this attracted local political attention and subsequent funding;

- in Germany, the work of Eurocounsel and its local consultants has been of particular significance in eastern Germany to ALI, the organisation in Thüringen responsible for counselling services there. As the German report states:

> *"the consultation in Phase I ... gave the opportunity to east German counsellors to obtain ideas for their own work from the experiences of their West German colleagues, from transferable examples of good working practices and also from the identification of mistakes which should not be repeated"* (Schumacher and Stiehr, 1993. Ref: 10, p.15);

-   in Ireland, the coinciding of the introduction of Eurocounsel at the same time as the PESP companies were being established is seen as having had a real impact on their development, particularly in areas where counselling services were limited or non-existent;

-   in Italy, the Eurocounsel programme has helped to focus attention on counselling and the development of counselling models, for example, the development of a proposal of plans for the provision of counselling services in the Friuli-Venezia-Giulia Region;

-   in Spain, the local consultants note that one of the main expectations hoped for from Eurocounsel was that it would be possible to link in with other EC programmes and initiatives to provide financial support for the technical issues associated with counselling (and there is some evidence that this has been possible in one or two instances, e.g. links with the NOW programme);

-   in the UK, the public Employment Service became directly involved in Eurocounsel through sponsorship of the meeting of senior government officials.

FINAL COMMENTS

The seven country reports produced by the Eurocounsel research team serve to highlight some of the key issues now emerging as to ways in which counselling services can be improved. It is interesting to note that the situation for the provision of services remains a dynamic one, constantly changing as economies, policies and institutions change and develop. The issues raised here, together with those in the next chapter (which focuses on the case studies and the transnational elements of the Eurocounsel programme) are drawn together in Chapter 5 on the findings and recommendations of Phase 2.

A key focus for Phase 2 of Eurocounsel was to increase the transnational dimension of the programme and the ways in which this has been done are commented on in the next chapter.

4   ISSUES EMERGING FROM THE CASE STUDIES   AND THE TRANSNATIONAL ELEMENTS OF PHASE 2

INTRODUCTION

This chapter describes the processes involved and the outcomes from the collation of the case studies portfolio and the three transnational elements of the programme:

-       the meeting of senior government officials (January 1993);

-       the pilot programme of study visits (January - May 1993); and

-       the Eurocounsel conference (May 1993).

EUROCOUNSEL CASE STUDIES

Preparation and Compilation

An important outcome of the action research in the second stage of Eurocounsel was the compilation of twenty-one case studies, three each from the countries participating in the programme. These were prepared according to case study guidelines agreed with all the local consultants. The outline for this format and a sample case study produced to illustrate for the consultants the sort of content and layout which was sought, is given in the appendices. (Appendix 3)

In November 1992, the selection of case studies by each consultant was discussed and agreed. It was confirmed that each of the three case studies written up by each consultants should highlight a different aspect of counselling, either in terms of its access, process, or outcomes, or in terms of the function it served i.e. solving, coping, or prevention. It was also agreed that different target groups might be examined, e.g. workers recently made redundant or women returners. Each consultant then put forward their proposed selection of three-four case studies and these were placed in a matrix which screened for access, process, or outcome and solving, coping or prevention, and by target group. As a result of this exercise, and discussion of the various case study proposals suggested, a matrix balanced in terms of aspects and functions of counselling, and by target group, was constructed and agreed.

The overall aim in researching and documenting the case studies was to compile a booklet which would provide examples of the many different innovative ways in which counselling is offered and provided. The booklet is intended to be a tool for promoting awareness and interest in the variety of counselling activity which is being undertaken throughout a number of European countries and to generate ideas, contacts, and discussion.

The case studies were completed by the time of the Eurocounsel conference in Dublin in May 1993, and were available, in the form of a draft portfolio, at that conference. The draft portfolio was well received and interest was expressed from a number of individuals and organisations in the content of the case studies. The final edited version of the portfolio is now completed and will be published by the Foundation. (7)

The list of each of the twenty-one case studies, by title, and function, is included in the case study publication and has been included here as one of the appendices simply for information. Further detailed information on the case studies is best obtained by reading the booklet.

LESSONS FROM THE CASE STUDIES

In this section of the report however it is considered important to refer to some of the significant factors which have emerged from the case studies because these have a direct bearing on other issues commented on in this report.

Within each trinity of case studies the participating countries all exhibit their own particular economic and social characteristics, but the growth in attention to, and the recognition of the importance of guidance and counselling as an increasingly powerful weapon in the fight against long-term unemployment, is significant and to be welcomed.

A number of major and minor strands emerged from these studies which are believed to be worth noting as perhaps offering signals about the way counselling is developing within Europe.

Counselling for Workers under Threat of Redundancy: Partnership approaches

This first major strand which emerged from the studies is that there seems to be an increasing interest in countries from the north and south of Europe in involving employers and government in new ways of addressing the needs of workers under threat of redundancy or recently dismissed. Denmark, Austria and Italy offer examples of innovative and dynamic approaches to addressing these problems, using counselling processes in order to try to prevent workers becoming long term unemployed. Although each case study reflects the different political and economic situation in each country, they all demonstrate the strengths of a partnership approach which involves workers, employers, trade unions and government agencies in coping with economic and social change.

Partnership approaches whereby both governmental and non-governmental organisations come together to develop and provide counselling services are also in evidence in Denmark and Ireland.

Counselling targeted on specific groups

The development of specific targeted provision for counselling particular groups of unemployed people is the second major strand which is evident in a number of the case studies. Ireland, Austria, Germany and the UK all offer examples of approaches to working with women wishing to enter or return to the workplace taking into account the particular needs of the clients. The UK study for example concentrates on Asian women in Bradford and highlights the very specific needs which ethnic minorities might have for counselling. Two cases also offer interesting approaches to dealing with special needs groups. One of the Austrian cases studies describes a system of counselling for employees and job seekers who have suffered mental health problems, whilst a Spanish case study outlines the very real difficulties and needs facing the mentally disabled in an economically disadvantaged area of southern Spain.

Counselling for Individual Choice and Control

Counselling models aimed at enabling individuals to make choices and increase control over their lives thereby moving away from a concept of the unemployed person as "powerless victim", is the third significant strand which has come out of the case studies. The guidance shop in Scotland; the peer group counselling in Denmark; the self-help youth organisation in Spain and the self-motivated information seeking system in the former East Germany demonstrate a variety of ways in which individuals are being encouraged and assisted towards self-empowerment. (Of course it is true to say that all of the case studies mentioned aim to assist individuals to develop and make choices, these highlighted here simply illustrate some innovative ways in which this is being approached).

A number of other points of significance emerge from an analysis of the case studies and these are highlighted below:

*   a growing move away from regarding unemployed people as a separate and stigmatised group was recorded in the cases from Austria, Denmark, and Ireland;

*   a recognition that counselling which is focused on career and labour market issues should also examine the overall context of the clients circumstances, including for instance their psychosocial needs, and address these also, was mentioned in cases from Austria, Ireland and Denmark.

*   the issue of voluntarism versus compulsion in labour market counselling and the effect of compulsion on the "client-centred" ethos of counselling was raised in most of the case studies. The majority of case studies described non-governmental agencies rather than public employment service agencies, and regarded the voluntarism ethos which they offered as one of their strengths.

*   the importance of networking and of public relations or marketing in order to persuade funding bodies and the public of the validity of counselling, particularly for vulnerable groups, was stressed in case studies from Austria, Denmark, and Ireland. Ireland highlighted the lack of networking as a problem in one of the case studies.

*   the Irish and Danish cases drew attention to the importance of taking the counselling to the client, in order to overcome both geographical and psychological problems which clients may experience in accessing counselling.

*   the need for an awareness of all the training/work placement and programme opportunities available, and an ability on the part of counselling staff to act as brokers between individuals seeking assistance and relevant agencies and projects came through in case studies from Italy, Germany, the UK, and Denmark.

*   ongoing counselling provision, i.e. the offer of continuing counselling for people once they are placed in training or work, was highlighted as a need in case studies from Spain and Ireland.

*   the importance of personal development planning being available for individuals who wanted it emerged from case studies in Germany, Ireland, and Spain.

*   the lack of resources or the instability of resources for counselling was reported in case studies, particularly those concerning counselling for targeted groups, in Austria, UK, and Germany.

The case studies offer a sample of current activity in guidance and counselling for unemployed people or those at risk of becoming unemployed within seven European countries, and they serve to highlight some issues which may find reflection in the experiences of other practitioners. Most of the examples are of counselling agencies which are funded by the state, acting as intermediaries for provision. Taken together with the range of other work which has been carried out during the course of Phase 2 of Eurocounsel, they help to fill in some of the detail of the overall picture of counselling in European countries which is now emerging.

MEETING OF SENIOR GOVERNMENT OFFICIALS

As part of the transnational element in Phase 2 of Eurocounsel it was decided to convene a meeting of "policy makers" who consisted of senior government officials mainly from public employment services.   Representatives from eight countries attended: Austria, Denmark, Germany, Ireland, Italy, Netherlands, Sweden and the U.K. The meeting was held in January 1993 in Edinburgh and was sponsored jointly by the Foundation and the U.K.'s Employment Service. A full report of the meeting has been compiled. (5)

The aim of the meeting was to allow government officials with responsibility in this area to identify and discuss key issues relating to ways in which counselling services can be improved.   During the course of the two day event, which was facilitated by the Eurocounsel programme co-ordinators Blake Stevenson Ltd, the following elements were covered:

-      a presentation of the findings of the first phase of Eurocounsel;

-      an opportunity for each participant who attended to make an input about issues relating to the provision of counselling services in their country;

-      small group and plenary sessions to allow participants to discuss some of the key issues identified in more depth.

The issues which were given fuller consideration during the meeting were as follows:

- is it helpful or not to link the payment of benefits with the provision of counselling (i.e. where there is an element of compulsion)?

- how can we measure quality in the services?

- the issues around early intervention (i.e. preventive counselling);

- the design of a high quality counselling system for the 1990s;

- making the case for counselling; and

- counselling in the changing labour market context.

A summary of the discussion which took place around each of these is given below.

Is it helpful to link benefits to the provision of counselling?

It was recognised at the meeting that there is disagreement about this issue of whether it is helpful or not to link benefits to the provision of counselling. Some of those present thought that the linking of counselling to the provision of unemployment benefits is definitely harmful and unhelpful while others thought that an element of compulsion is useful for people who might otherwise not approach counselling services due to lack of motivation or confidence. This led to a discussion as to whether there is a hard-core of unemployed people who are unlikely ever to work again for whom it is not appropriate to offer counselling and that perhaps they should be removed from the register or simply allowed to continue receiving benefits without having to be involved in counselling or other labour market measures.

It was agreed that there are no easy solutions, or right answers, to these questions and that the route adopted will depend very much on the political, economic and social circumstances of each country.

How can we measure quality in services?

The outcomes of the discussion around how best to measure quality were presented under three main headings:

-       the need first of all to define what we mean by quality;

-       the importance of taking account both of subjective and objective factors and the need to measure both of these accurately;

-       the need to assess the expectations of the different players involved: users (employers and job seekers); funders; and counselling practitioners.

Issues around early intervention

Three main issues were identified in the discussions around the importance of early intervention:

-       the need to produce measures to analyse the different effects of providing counselling earlier or later so that more evidence is available on this issue;

-       the importance of identifying any special needs which the individual may have before unemployment begins;

-       achieving a balance between where the responsibility of the individual to take action and those of the state to provide services begins and ends.

Designing a high quality counselling system for the 1990s

One of the small group sessions during the meeting designed what they perceived as a high quality counselling system provided by a public employment service for the 1990s. A flow chart of how this system would operate was prepared and is shown in Figure 1. The key points to note about the system are as follows:

Users:	anyone making a transition from and/or to education/training/employment.
Providers:	the Employment Service, contracted delivery agents and complementary providers.
Aims:	Contributing to social stability and labour market efficiency by giving priority to people most in need, in an environment of continuing restructuring and high unemployment.
Desired outcomes:	1. the ability for people to place themselves correctly in the labour market and social context;
	2. making people capable of deciding their own future and directions forward.

The service is designed based on the principles of respect for the individual and enabling people to take decisions for themselves.

FIGURE 1
A COUNSELLING SYSTEM FOR THE 1990s

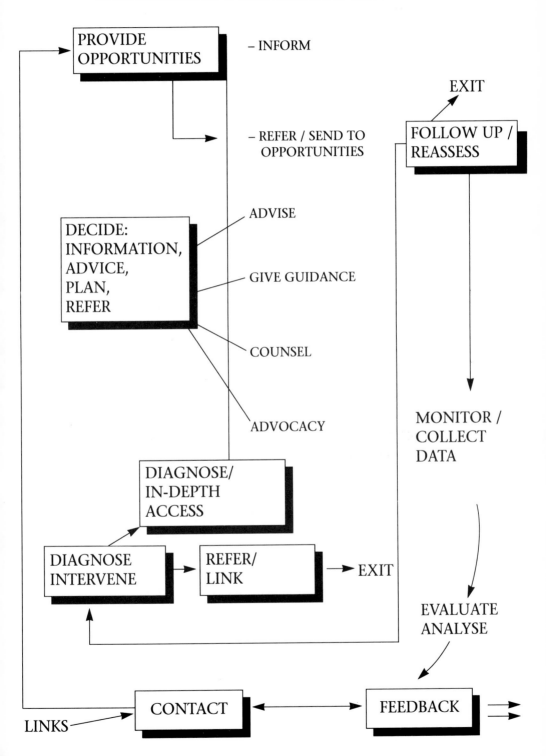

The case for counselling

It was agreed that with mounting pressure on resources there will be an increasing need to be able to make the case for counselling convincingly to politicians and other policy makers. This will require effective measurements and evaluations to be made so that the evidence to support the arguments is in place. It was recognised that what is considered to be an effective measurement will vary because the outcomes desired from counselling services also vary according to whether you are a funder, a client or practitioner within the service. Sometimes these desired outcomes will be in conflict with each other which will influence measurement. For example, short-term versus long-term results as in the case where it may be possible to get numbers off the unemployed register (short term outcome sought by the funder) to the detriment of the "right" job/training being found (longer term goal for the client). It is a question of deciding priorities in terms of outcomes sought: if getting the "right" job/training is the priority then it may take longer but the result will be more people staying in their jobs for longer.

The changing context of the labour market and the future of work

While accepting that counselling cannot provide the solution for all the ills of the labour market a number of points were made as to ways in which counselling services can play a greater role in this area. These included the following:

- counselling should focus on empowering individuals while recognising the tension between this and meeting the needs of society i.e. for skills;

- discussion as to whether counselling should be compulsory for the unemployed or not, with acceptance that there are differing views as to the answer to this question;

- agreement that the nature of work must change in order to allow for more rotation of the work which is available and to allow for periods of leave out of the labour market, for voluntary work, education etc. With the increasing flexibility and mobility in the labour market and the growth in short-term contracts the need for counselling services for all adults will increase.

CONCLUSIONS FROM THE MEETING

Some of the key issues which emerged during this meeting are summarised in the paragraphs which follow.

There are a lot of common issues

Despite the fact that there are differences between the counselling services offered in each country, the meeting highlighted the fact that there are also a lot of similarities. One of the common issues which countries share is the shortage of resources and the need to persuade key policy makers and politicians of the effectiveness of counselling. The participants agreed that it is important to have the opportunities to share new ideas and innovative developments in transnational meetings because otherwise there is a danger that the potential of counselling as a measure to assist in the reintegration of unemployed people and the reduction of social exclusion will be reduced.

Integrated counselling

Counselling services need to be offered which meet every aspect of the needs of the unemployed individual including personal and social as well as labour market issues. They should start with preventive work and continue for a period after the unemployed person has secured employment or become engaged in training/education. Counselling services should be available where appropriate to employers. Both employers and trade unions should be involved in the provision of services. Counselling should be integrated into regional economic policy instead of being a mere instrument of social change.

Counselling for the employed as well as the unemployed

This is a difficult issue to raise at a time when the arguments to maintain services for the unemployed, let alone the employed, are having to be made. With rising unemployment there are severe pressures on the resources available which impact on the provision of counselling. Nevertheless it is recognised that there is much to be gained by offering counselling services to all adults of working age. This, it is thought, will assist not only the individuals concerned but also the labour market itself in terms of its dynamism.

Counselling is about personal development and opportunity awareness

The outcomes of counselling have to combine both personal development (the ability to take decisions with confidence and self-awareness) with an awareness of the opportunities available in terms of employment, training and education and other forms of activity. Being better able to measure the outcomes of counselling will enable the services to be improved as well as assisting in making the case for such services to be maintained and extended.

The need for work at national and transnational levels

The meeting in Edinburgh was regarded as a success by those who attended it. It shows that by creating the opportunity for ideas to be shared at transnational level, such as on this occasion, national practices are also affected as those who participate are able to reflect more fully on their own situation by comparing it to others. As one of the participants summed it up:

> "..the problems for counselling call for both national and transnational developing actions...The Eurocounsel seminar in Edinburgh is very important to discuss and point out the central issues for this transnational work. We need networks at different levels to build an exchange of knowledge and common projects." (Stig Sirich Andersen, Denmark. Ref: 5)

THE PILOT PROGRAMME OF STUDY VISITS

As part of the transnational element of Phase 2 of Eurocounsel, a small pilot programme of study visits was organised by the programme co-ordinators involving counselling practitioners from the twelve local labour market participating areas in Eurocounsel. The purpose of the programme was to allow these practitioners the opportunity to visit another country in order to learn more about a particular aspect of counselling in a different European context.

A total of eighteen people took part in the study visits funded by Eurocounsel together with the participants' own organisations and, in the case of the Austrian participants, the Austrian government. Each person visited a host organisation in one of the other participating local labour market areas. The participants indicated both their preferred subject area and ideal destination and where possible these were met. The topics which they focused on included the following:

- group counselling;

- counselling for target groups;

- outreach counselling;

- counselling linked to job opportunities;

- preventative counselling;

- redundancy counselling;

- counselling linked to learning and education;

- the training of counsellors.

There are a number of issues arising out of this pilot programme. These concern the outcomes for the participants themselves, issues concerned with the organisational process involved, the benefits of such study programmes and the results in relation to the Eurocounsel programme.

Outcomes for the participants

Each participant was asked to write a short report after the visit had taken place. Many of these indicate clearly the learning outcomes for the individuals concerned. These include specific examples such as the Austrian who went to Ireland and decided that more needs to be done in Austria in relation to counselling young people in rural areas about the opportunities available to them. Another example is that of the Irish visitors who went to Denmark and have returned to Ireland and followed up what they learnt by holding a meeting with FAS, the Irish manpower agency, about developing closer and more regular contact with unemployed people to inform them of work and training schemes.

The organisational process

Due to pressure on resources and time the organisation for the study visits was purposely kept to a minimum. Blake Stevenson as the Eurocounsel co-ordinators had responsibility for the overall co-ordination and were assisted in each country by the Eurocounsel local consultants. This process depended very much on the co-operation of host agencies which was excellent. However in terms of future such organisation, it meant that the co-ordinators had little control of what was planned for each visitor and so there was an element of luck involved which in an ideal situation, with fuller resources would be avoided.

The restricted resources did not allow for full preparation for each visitor and this was undertaken on an ad hoc basis again relying on the co-operation of the host agencies.

Wherever possible, accommodation was provided by an employee of the host organisation. This enhanced the benefits of the study visit and has been commented upon favourably in several of the participants' reports. It meant that the experience was not restricted to a limited number of official contacts.

The benefits (and drawbacks) of this study visit programme

This pilot programme of study visits is the first time the Foundation has been involved in such a programme and has been seen to be a useful additional element in the action research process which is the method used in Eurocounsel.

The main drawback to the pilot study visit programme was the restriction of resources of time and budget. This meant that the normal thorough preparation both of the participants and the receiving organisations, which is an important element of running such programmes, had to be undertaken on a more ad hoc basis than is ideal. Having said this, the restriction on resources may have encouraged the high sense of involvement and commitment from the participants, the local consultants and the host agencies.

One of the benefits is that the participants gain specific new ideas which they can then pass on to others on their return. The Irish and the German visits produced this kind of result. Another direct benefit is that those involved meet potential partners for future transnational collaboration which is an increasingly important need in Europe. The Danish and Irish visit reports have indicated that there might be some future collaboration.

Apart from these direct benefits, the key result in any study visit of this kind is the opportunity it allows those participating to stand back a bit from their own everyday situation and reflect on it. Visiting other counselling services in a different country gives the opportunity to compare and contrast practices and ideas: most often there will not be directly transferable ideas to take home but the differences of approach and ideas will stimulate new thinking about the person's own agency and practices.

The issues for Eurocounsel emerging from this process

There are a number of issues for Eurocounsel emerging from this study visit process. These include the following:

-       the study visit programme has enhanced the transnational element of Phase 2 of Eurocounsel; many of those who took part in the visits also attended the conference in Dublin in May and were able to contribute more to the discussions there as a result of their visits;

-       this pilot programme has been a cost effective one, due largely to the willing co-operation of host agencies and participants;

-       there is a need to examine whether there can be opportunities to continue such a programme, possibly on an informal basis, in the future.

THE EUROCOUNSEL CONFERENCE

The Eurocounsel conference was held in May 1993 in Dublin. The aims of the conference were as follows:

-       to promote the exchange of information on advice, information, guidance and counselling services in the context of the development of the labour market and the reduction of unemployment;

-       to disseminate and discuss the results of Phase I and 2 of the Foundation's Eurocounsel programme on counselling and long-term unemployment;

-   to develop proposals and recommendations to improve and enhance the quality and effectiveness of counselling, information, advice and guidance services in the labour market.

Around 100 delegates attended the conference from countries within the EC as well as those outwith it, including Sweden, Finland, USA, and the CSFR. A full report of the conference proceedings has been prepared. (6)

The findings of Phases I and 2 were presented by the Foundation's Senior Research Manager responsible for Eurocounsel and the programme co-ordinator from Blake Stevenson Ltd. Other European organisations and programmes with an interest in this area also gave presentations on their work including CEDEFOP, the European organisation responsible for the development of vocational training, PETRA, the programme which promotes vocational training for young people and the European Commission's ERGO 2 programme, which focuses on long-term unemployment. Conference delegates also heard about counselling provision in varied labour market situations in France, Sweden, Italy and Ireland. Three of the case studies which have been researched during Phase 2 were given as illustrations of ways in which counselling services are being improved.

During the first part of the conference the delegates met in small working groups to discuss their views as to the main gaps in services at present. These discussions focused around a paper which had been written by the programme co-ordinators and distributed prior to the conference. There was general agreement that the gaps identified in this paper were correct and so it is included in the Appendices for reference. (See Appendix 2).

The section of the conference which examined ways in which counselling services could be improved was focused around working groups made up of conference delegates from the following areas:

-   government officials;

-   employers;

-   practitioners and representatives of users;

-   European-wide organisations.

Each of these groups produced some important recommendations as to ways in which counselling services can be improved. Together with some stimulating inputs about the future for counselling service provision made on the last day of the conference by speakers from the social partners (UNICE and ETUC), the ILO, the International Association for Educational and Vocation Guidance, and the European Network of the Unemployed, they form the basis for the key issues emerging from the conference which are described below.

Key issues and recommendations emerging from the conference

Many of the issues which arose during the conference sessions, reflect those which are found in the country reports. In addition some important recommendations and suggestions as to ways to improve services were made and these are presented here and commented on further in Chapter 5.

Preventive counselling

The importance of preventive counselling as a form of early intervention was endorsed by the conference delegates. In particular it was suggested that more could be done to offer such counselling services to small and medium sized enterprises which know that they are going to have to lay off employees. The role which trade unions can play in encouraging and supporting this form of counselling provision was stressed.

Information

The need for up to date, accurate and practical information about the local labour market and the general range of opportunities for unemployed people was highlighted many times during the conference. There is a need to examine both the effective gathering of information and also its dissemination to those who will use it. One suggestion put forward was that in a local or regional area there should be one main body charged with distributing the information to the network.

In terms of the future it was suggested that this area of information provision will alter radically given the impact of new technology. The problems in particular of rural areas in accessing information may be reduced. However the question of how to manage information and who controls it will remain.

The involvement of users

Throughout the conference the importance of user involvement in identifying needs and being able to contribute directly to the ways in which services are organised was emphasized. It was suggested that further research is needed to examine the ways in which such involvement can take place. Linked to this, the need for users to increase their own formal organisation in the form of unions was raised.

Resources to allow the organisations of the unemployed to make effective representation at European level are needed: one delegate compared the resources which the farmers' lobby has to those which the unemployed have and pointed out that there are many more unemployed people.

Access to services

It was suggested that it is important to provide informal as well as formal access to services. It was considered that decentralisation can assist in opening up access to services, although recognising that the need for effective linkages between services at local level will be essential in order to avoid confusion to the user.

Counselling for the whole person

The need to provide counselling services which meet the needs of the "whole person" was emphasized in particular by contributors from Austria, Ireland and France. This is to recognize the fact that for most unemployed people there are a range of needs not just those which relate specifically to gaining employment. These include all aspects of life which not having a job impinge on: financial, personal confidence, status and social relations.

Multi- disciplinary teams

The suggestion was made at the conference for the development of more multi-disciplinary teams, which relates to the point above to meet the needs of the whole person. These teams would recognise that in providing services for the unemployed a whole range of skills and understanding are needed which it is unlikely will be found in one person. This would allow for the development of a genuine client-centred approach.

Counselling related to opportunities outwith the first labour market

It is apparent that the demand for labour within the traditional labour market is not sufficient in many parts of Europe to meet the supply of labour available and that new opportunities are needed if those who are unemployed are not simply to be ignored and socially excluded. Such opportunities can include job creation, either through self employment or small business development, voluntary work and work placements.

It was suggested that counselling can have a role to play in assisting people to become involved in the local development process which examines what opportunities can be opened up.

Compulsion, benefits and counselling

There was a strong sense on the part of some of the conference delegates that counselling services should be kept separate from the provision of benefits. This is because it is perceived that an element of compulsion in relation to benefits may remove the possibility for a client-centred approach to be taken. The opposite point of view was also put forward which is that without an element of compulsion some of those who are in need of counselling assistance will not be motivated enough to come to services.

The role of employers

Several specific suggestions as to ways to further involve employers in this area were made. These included the need for closer links between employers and public employment agencies so that each could understand the other more clearly. It was thought that the ways in which employers notify vacancies should be re-examined and that they should be encouraged to advertise all vacancies through the public employment services. This will help to avoid the possible discrimination which can take place for those who are unemployed where vacancies are advertised by word of mouth.

It is important to alter the perceptions which many employers have of long-term unemployed people. One way to do this will be to encourage more employers to offer work placements to those who are unemployed and to support with the appropriate services both the employers and the unemployed, during the placement, in this process.

Training for practitioners

The need for high quality, appropriate training for counselling practitioners was emphasized several times during the conference. Creating opportunities for practitioners to meet and exchange ideas both within an area, between areas within a country and between different countries can contribute to "training" and the professional development of those involved.

The role of partnerships

Partnerships between the public, private and voluntary sectors, often involving the social partners, are increasingly found in the establishment and delivery of counselling services. Trade union and employers' representatives at the conference both expressed interest and commitment in finding ways to improve counselling services.

Measuring outcomes and evaluating services

Although delegates agreed that this was an essential area if services are to be improved, it was thought that further research is needed to develop practical ways in which this can be done. It was agreed that such evaluations will facilitate making the case for counselling to policy makers and politicians at a time when there is increasing pressure on resources.

Resources and budgets

A practical suggestion made at the conference was to decentralise resources and budgets to regional level by allocating block resources and allowing those at this level to make decisions as to how best to use them to meet the counselling needs of the people in their area. Linked to the earlier comment about the involvement of the unemployed in identifying needs, this decentralisation of resources would ideally allow for those who are affected by unemployment to have a meaningful say in the way in which services are provided.

Networks

Throughout the conference the complexity and range of counselling services were highlighted. The need for networks at local and regional levels was clearly identified as one way to improve services through better co-ordination and collaboration. Networking can assist in improving the sharing of information and in the spread of good practice. Some countries, such as Denmark, have already recognised this need and have established formal networks.

It was emphasized that a form of superstructure is not what is wanted. The involvement of the users in these networks was again stressed.

A European Network?

Towards the end of the conference the suggestion was made (from the government officials' working group) for a European Network of counselling practitioners and researchers in this area. This idea gained general approval at the conference and it will be important to investigate ways in which it might be taken forward.

Conclusions

The conference was a successful event and allowed a number of important issues to be discussed as well as practical recommendations to be made. One of the interesting features is that although the range of services and the forms of provision vary from country to country there is such consensus as to the priority gaps and issues to be tackled in bringing about improvements to services. The specific recommendations for ways forward are incorporated into the chapter on findings and recommendations of this report.

5 FINDINGS AND RECOMMENDATIONS FROM PHASE 2 OF EUROCOUNSEL

Introduction

As has been shown in chapters 3 and 4 of this report, Phase 2 of Eurocounsel has produced a wealth of results. These results come from the work of the local consultants and from the contributions made by participants at the various transnational events which have been held. The aim of this chapter is to synthesise the main findings of all this work and to add a commentary. During this phase it has been possible to begin to identify ways in which we can shape and improve counselling services for the future. The second part of this chapter offers specific recommendations as to ways in which counselling services can be made more effective.

Reflection on the aims of the programme

The aims of the programme are to improve the quality and effectiveness of information, advice, guidance and counselling services in relation to the prevention and solution of long-term unemployment. Much work was done in Phase 1 of Eurocounsel to understand what the deficiencies in those services are and this understanding has been deepened in Phase 2 and has given a clearer vision as to what is needed to develop and improve services and what the potential for barriers to this are. It is evident that the aims of the programme as a whole remain highly relevant as unemployment rises and the role which counselling has to play increases rather than diminishes.

The provision of counselling services relating to unemployment is complex but there are common issues.

The work of Phase 2 of Eurocounsel has reinforced the fact that the issues involved in the provision of counselling services relating to unemployment are complex. There is, if anything, increasing diversity in the range of services on offer and at the same time a growing demand for them. However the transnational element of this phase has highlighted the fact that there are very many common issues across the countries involved, despite the differences between their systems, and that many of the current gaps in services are similar.

FINDINGS

Commentary on the results of the local consultants' work, the case studies and the transnational elements of Phase 2.

There are some issues which were raised in the earlier chapters which require further comment here as part of the overall findings of this phase of the Eurocounsel programme. The findings are structured according to the analytical framework which has been used throughout Phases 1 and 2 of the Eurocounsel programme. This involves an examination of issues relating to the national context and systems in each participating country, and a focus on issues of access to counselling services, the processes involved and the outcomes of counselling provision. It is recognised that issues do not only belong to one or other of these groupings and that there are many linkages between them. For example, the institutional structure of public services affects who provides what services and with what objectives, and the outcomes are affected by conditions of access and the content of the service itself.

CONTEXT AND SYSTEMS

The findings from the participating countries relating to the context and systems cover issues at national level which impinge on counselling provision. The results from chapters 3 and 4 are the starting point for these findings, and where appropriate, further commentary is added.

The effects of rising unemployment on counselling provision

Phase 2 of Eurocounsel has seen a rise in unemployment in all the Member States. Between countries however, and within them, the patterns of unemployment vary considerably. For example, in relation to the seven countries participating in Eurocounsel, the highest level of unemployment is in Spain at 21% and the lowest in Germany (5.5%). Within these figures lie many further variations linked to a country's demographic patterns as well as previous unemployment and long-term unemployment rates.

A general finding is that as unemployment rises the demand for information, advice, guidance and counselling also increases at a time when it is harder to find jobs, so that the practitioner's work is made more difficult.

Pressure on resources

Linked to the problem of rising unemployment, and of great significance to the provision of counselling, is the pressure on public expenditure and resources in many countries. Again the extent of the problem varies from country to country, but the pressure is felt to some degree by all the countries which have participated in Eurocounsel. This problem of resources is one which affects all aspects of counselling services: access to them, the processes involved and the outcomes. It will be referred to many times throughout this chapter.

One of the issues for resourcing is whether users should be charged for the service they receive or not. It links in with points made earlier in this report concerning the need to balance the responsibility of the individual for their own development with intervention by the State. Where resources are restricted it will perhaps be helpful to prioritise free services to those who are most disadvantaged. For example, those in employment could pay for such services.

There are indications that in some countries such as Spain and Italy, that there is competition for resources between what are perceived as economic and social measures. For example, the work of local economic development agencies may be more likely to be prioritised to receive funding rather than the more human and "soft" measures such as counselling. There may be a need to rectify the balance and develop closer links between these two areas. This is particularly so, now that a Council resolution has been passed, recognising the importance of investment in vocational education and training. (Ref: 25) Counselling and guidance are an essential part of making this investment operate as effectively and efficiently as possible.

The whole question of resource allocation and the determination of priorities can be assisted by close collaboration between public authorities, the social partners, practitioners and users. There is also scope, as highlighted at the Eurocounsel conference, for greater local or regional autonomy in determining priorities.

A general move towards decentralisation

Across Europe there appears to be a general move towards decentralisation. This is true even in countries such as Spain and Italy which previously had a stronger centralist approach. For counselling services, this raises the possibility for closer attention to local needs and may increase the number of services available. However, the problem of resources remains and creates an ever greater need for better co-ordination of all the providers including effective local networks between them.

In addition to this geographical decentralisation there is a form of institutional decentralisation through the transfer of service provision from the public sector to agencies acting for them as intermediaries. This development of intermediaries has been discussed earlier in this report (p.31).

The need for counselling services separate from benefits provision

One of the debates which has arisen during Phase 2 of Eurocounsel is that of the issue of compulsory counselling linked to the provision and administration of unemployment benefits and subsidies and whether this is helpful or not. It is likely that in any provision of benefits there will be an element of information, advice, guidance or counselling and that these are linked in some countries to the eligibility to collect benefit. It may be that for some people some form of compulsory counselling is beneficial. However, this does not detract from the need to have separate neutral counselling provision available which is more likely to be able to provide a fully client-centred service. Such separate services are important to users both in terms of access (on a voluntary basis) and the processes involved.

The potential for positive developments in counselling provision

The background of economic crisis (and in some countries, such as Italy, of political and institutional crisis) means that there are new opportunities to be seized. In times of difficulty people will often search for new solutions: "necessity is the mother of invention". In some countries this may mean radical change is possible and in most it will mean that change of some sort will be required. This has practical implications for the provision of counselling. While always emphasizing that counselling itself is not and cannot be a solution to unemployment, it has been demonstrated during the work of Eurocounsel to date that it has important roles to play both in the prevention of long-term unemployment and in assisting people to find jobs, training and learning opportunities or ways to create their own employment. If, as seems likely, our labour markets continue to move towards ever increasing flexibility and mobility, then the role of counselling will increase rather then diminish.

The opportunities and challenges are to find ways in which counselling services can operate most effectively both to assist those who are unemployed and those who are currently in work.

The importance of partnerships

There is evidence as has been shown earlier in this report that counselling is being increasingly provided by partnerships between government, private and voluntary sector bodies. With the increasing complexity of counselling provision, the pressure on resources and the continuing rise in demand from users, the role for such partnerships will become more important.

The European dimension

With the creation of the Single Market in 1992 new opportunities are opening up for employment within a European labour market. Counselling can assist individuals to tap into this potential market although there is a need to make connections between it and local labour markets. Within this area there can be new opportunities for those who are disadvantaged in the labour market, to travel and have work experiences elsewhere which has been seen to be beneficial in terms of renewing self-confidence and motivation.

Counselling provision in areas of low demand for labour

One of the key concerns throughout Phase 2 of Eurocounsel as unemployment rises has been what counselling services are most appropriate to offer in areas where there is low demand for labour, such as the southern parts of Italy and Spain, eastern Germany and rural Ireland. In Phase 1 of Eurocounsel three different functions of counselling were described: solving; coping; and prevention. The coping function was seen to be particularly applicable in such areas of low demand for labour. It has both reactive and pro-active connotations. As a reactive measure it assists the individual to "cope" with their situation. However, it also has an important pro-active function: it can assist the user to create their own opportunities and to be instrumental in developing their own solutions to the problem of long-term unemployment. Self-help initiatives, supported by professional counsellors, and services which allow for full involvement of the users in their design will be particularly effective in this respect.

The functions of solving, coping, *activating* and prevention

For reasons of clarity it may be useful to add a fourth function to the three existing functions of counselling which have been identified. This allows for the re-active and pro-active aspects of coping to be separated out and gives a clearer definition to pro-active coping, that of "activation". The activating function of counselling is concerned with all opportunities not directly related to matching/solving the demands of the primary labour market. (The primary labour market is defined as jobs which are provided by established employers in the private, public or voluntary sectors, who buy the labour of individuals for a wage). These other opportunities include:

-    self-employment;

-    employment creation associated with local economic development (which will involve new business development which in time may become part of the primary labour market);

-    social employment (including temporary work schemes for community benefit "enterprises d'insertion" community co-operatives and businesses);

-    voluntary work;

-    training and learning opportunities.

Counselling provision related to increasing flexibility in the labour market

Within the primary labour market there is increasing flexibility demanded of workers by employers. Part-time work, short-term contracts, technological developments and issues of mobility increase the need for individuals to have access to counselling and guidance to assist them to develop their own potential and to make the right choices with regard to training, education and work. Many people will find themselves in precarious employment which increases their need for counselling and guidance. At the same time, the demand for improved education and training for all adults will also affect the demand for counselling services, particularly as people come to recognise for themselves what it has to offer. This highlights the need for counselling services to be available to all adults and will be referred to again in a later paragraph.

A vision for counselling linked to a broader understanding of and meaning for the "labour market".

With 17 million currently unemployed in Europe it is clear that the demand for labour in the traditional primary labour market is at present lower than the supply of labour. In trying to come to terms with this problem of unemployment different approaches are being taken. At European level the approach is to find ways to intensify job creation within economic growth as described in the Commission of the European Communities' Employment Framework document in May 1993 (Ref: 17). A similar strategy in the United States has led to a larger amount of lower paid jobs. Others, such as the Danish, are concerned with creating a wider range of opportunities in order to keep those who are unemployed active. This is not a new approach but the political attention which it is receiving is new. There are also more radical discussions as to ways in which paid work can be redefined and more evenly distributed.

It is important to relate these developments in the debates about labour to the area of counselling provision in order to broaden our understanding of what is possible. In relation to the provision of counselling services to prevent and find solutions to long-term unemployment, it is perhaps helpful to take the broadest meaning of the "labour market" rather than simply the traditional primary labour markets. This broader approach might be usefully re-named, for example the "labour field". It might be helpful if this meaning could be more generally used as it recognises that many forms of labour are required in order for societies to work effectively: of course, to have real meaning for those who are currently unemployed, all the activities outlined below would require to have some form of payment or for it to be accepted that everyone undertakes a mixture of them in order to best meet the needs of society and satisfy the individual's need for some form of paid employment, e.g. most people will have a portfolio of work which includes some paid work, caring for children or the elderly at home and some voluntary work. The outlets for labour include the following:

- jobs in the primary labour market;
- self employment;
- social employment (including temporary work schemes for community benefit "enterprises d'insertion" community co-operatives and businesses);
- employment creation linked to local economic development;
- voluntary work;
- caring work in the home (of children and increasingly elderly people).

The person supplying the labour for any of the above has training and education needs which have to be met if they are to perform their work effectively. They also require awareness of the opportunities which are available to them, an understanding of their own skills and aspirations and an ability to take decisions.

All of the above areas can be assisted by information, advice, guidance and counselling services. The approach which has been outlined above is a holistic one in terms of society's needs for labour. There has been much discussion in Phase 2 about meeting the needs of the individual person through counselling in a holistic way: it is important to address the needs of society for labour in a similarly holistic way. Counselling is centrally about assisting the individual but it is also about wider issues such as how individuals are enabled to contribute to society in ways best suited to their abilities and which support them to find a living.

If the above approach is followed then in addition to viewing counselling as a means to reintegrate those who have lost their paid jobs back into the labour market, counselling can be seen as a tool to assist in the prevention of social exclusion and to assist society gain the best from all of its members. It is similar to the "lifelong learning" maxim in that it broadens out the vision of what it is we are trying to achieve by offering such services. To sum up, the perceived roles for counselling services are closely linked to the ways in which work and labour are viewed in society.

The importance of counselling for all adults, throughout their working life.

It is clear that if the "labour field" approach is followed, of counselling being important in relation to all aspects of labour, that it is then important that *all* people interested in entering the labour market have access to it and not just those who are unemployed or at risk of becoming so. At present there tends to be better counselling and guidance provision within schools rather than for those who have left full-time education. Counselling and guidance can assist with the many transitions in and out of labour and with the development of each individual's potential linked to skills and training requirements. This has benefits not only for the individual in that it can help to prevent long-term unemployment and increase the likelihood of fulfilling potential, but it is also beneficial for society in that it acts as a lubricant in terms of maintaining individuals' flexibility and involvement in different labour outlets. This is not to deny that those who are long-term unemployed should not be given targeted assistance but is rather to stress that there will be less of those who find themselves in this position if a more holistic approach to the labour needs of society is taken. A recent working document on vocational guidance produced by the EC's Task Force on Human Resources identifies five reasons why such provision is important which are as follows:

-       as a key to the development of human resources;

-       as a lubricant of change;

-       as a facilitator of social equity;

-       as a partnership between different areas of activity;

-       as a stimulant for local and regional development.

A comprehensive model for counselling provision

Taking the above three paragraphs into account it is clear that there is an opportunity to develop a comprehensive model for counselling provision. This model would recognise that the opportunities to offer labour are many and that counselling can assist all adults to find the most appropriate jobs/training/unpaid activities to suit their own situation. It recognises that reintegration into the primary labour market is one of several positive outcomes of counselling provision.

It is important to stress however, that the success of this comprehensive system will depend in part on a change in attitude to the ways in which work and labour are viewed. It will only work if everyone participates and paid work is shared or redistributed or dramatically increased. The necessity for some form of paid labour remains for each individual. This model is one which hopefully moves away from a position of social exclusion for many towards a more equal distribution of labour and work sharing for all. Figure I illustrates this comprehensive model. It shows counselling as a core service which can support movement to and between a variety of labour related activities. Counselling can assist the transition between each of these activities as well as those who wish to progress within them or to enter them from having been unemployed. It can help individuals to make planned exits from labour activity (on retirement) and planned entry into it (on leaving school). It can also help in increasing mobility by providing guidance on all of these activities in other parts of Europe.

FIGURE 2
A COMPREHENSIVE COUNSELLING MODEL

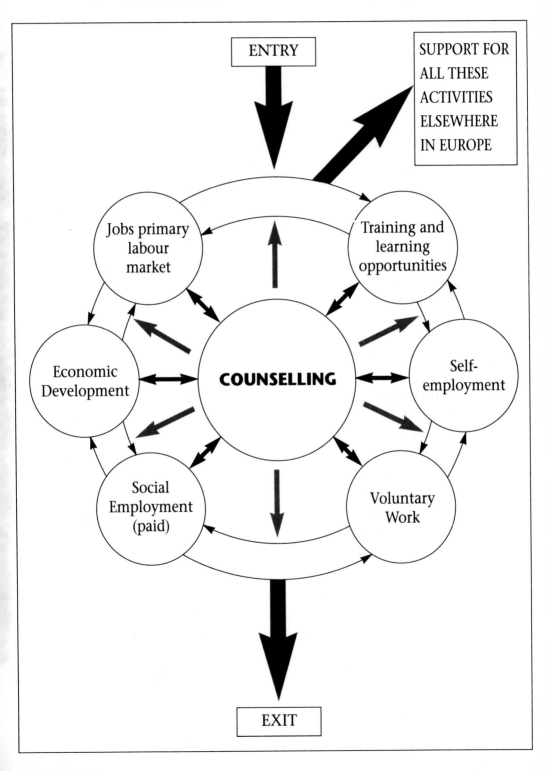

ACCESS

The effects of limited resources on access

There are many different kinds of issues to consider in relation to improving access to counselling services. These consist both of physical aspects as well as mental or psychological ones. Within the context of limited resources described earlier, access to services may be restricted by whether they exist or not and by the level of provision they are able to offer. While we have seen the development of counselling services in Phase 2 increase where none existed before, such as in Trieste in Italy, there have at the same time been reductions in the numbers of people offering counselling in other countries such as Germany due to the pressure on resources. Two further issues of access which relate to resourcing are whether services should be free or not and what kinds of eligibility criteria are imposed.

The different kinds of counselling related to issues of access

There are also issues of access linked to the type of counselling which is required. For example, it is often relatively easy to gain access to information whereas it may be more difficult (again due partly to issues of resourcing) to have one-to-one counselling as it takes more of a practitioner's time and requires someone with these skills. The growing use of new technology, which can meet more of the user's information needs, may serve to allow more resources to be devoted to the more costly one-to-one counselling services. Group counselling may serve as a less expensive form of provision than one-to-one counselling but retain some of the advantages of self-help counselling described in the paragraph below. It allows for peer support and may be less threatening for some users than the one-to-one situation.

Increased access via self-help initiatives

One way in which the problem of limited resources may be overcome and access to services increased is by the development of self-help initiatives. A number of these initiatives have been described in the local consultants' reports for Phase 2, for example in Denmark and Austria. These initiatives require different kinds of support from counselling practitioners, who may have further training needs to assist them in providing it. There are also drawbacks to this form of counselling in that inevitably there is a turnover of those who are involved in the initiative and this may cause fluctuations affecting both access to the service and the process of counselling itself.

Giving the user a clear understanding of what services have to offer

Psychological access can be increased if the user has a clear understanding of what the service has to offer. The development of guides or "user maps" in some countries, such as Denmark and the UK, is helpful in this respect. Services need to give attention to the forms of publicity they provide as these will all have bearing on the user's perceptions and expectations of them.

Outreach remains important

The issue of improving access to services through outreach work is important. There are interesting examples in Phase 2 of Eurocounsel in rural areas such as north Mayo in Ireland, as to ways to take services to where people live. The problems of outreach may be most obvious in rural areas but in urban areas too it is important to examine new ways to reach potential users. The development of high street shops in the UK which are independent and provide counselling and guidance services to all adults are a good example of this. Community-based provision is important too and can assist in overcoming some of the apprehension which may inhibit access for some individuals in dealing with government offices.

PROVISION AND PROCESS

The complexity of counselling provision

There are many complexities to the provision of counselling. Firstly, there are within the overall term "counselling" different kinds of service as has been identified in the definitions used throughout the Eurocounsel programme: information, advice, guidance and counselling itself. Individuals will have different needs in relation to each of these services according to their circumstances. One-to-one counselling will not be the most appropriate service at all times: accurate and relevant information can play just as important a role.

Secondly, counselling is provided by many different practitioners coming from a range of backgrounds. These include those engaged as:

- professional educational guidance workers;

- occupational counsellors;

- psychosocial counsellors;

- voluntary workers;

- practitioners involved via other labour market measures (such as training providers).

Some of these practitioners focus mainly on information provision, others on guidance and/or counselling per se. There are also those who work specifically with self-help groups. The training needs of this wide range of practitioners clearly vary too. As the numbers and types of providers increase so will the importance of making links between practitioners involved in the different sectors: public, private and voluntary.

The developing profession of "labour field" counsellors

In relation to the comprehensive counselling model for the whole labour market described earlier in this chapter, it appears that a new counselling professional is emerging who combines several of the elements described in the paragraph above. This person has to have a wide range of skills and abilities and as such the profession should be recognised within its own right as one of high status. The range of skills includes:

- ability to access and use information (about the labour market and education/training);

- high level general interpersonal skills;

- networking skills;

- counselling skills;

- "activating" skills;

- brokerage skills;

- ability to analyse and provide feedback to policy makers and providers on user's perceptions on systems of labour market measures;

-       ability to support self-help initiatives.

Not all of these will be found in one person and opportunities to develop multi-disciplinary teams should be identified. There will be a need for specialists in any of the above skill areas, e.g. in information, but there is also a need for generalists who can provide a range of these skills.

The importance of early intervention balanced with the need to target resources to those who are most disadvantaged

Phase 2 of Eurocounsel has provided several examples of early intervention and preventive counselling. Many of these are associated with large-scale industry restructuring such as in ex-coal fields or steel areas. The work of organisations such as British Coal Enterprise in the UK and the Austrian Arbeitsstiftung (Labour Foundations) are an important examples of this. Preventive counselling needs to be encouraged further and spread to involve more small and medium-sized companies. The importance of this early intervention is that it can help to prevent long-term unemployment and thereby be cost-effective in the longer term.

Resources have to be carefully balanced in order to provide early intervention and also to target assistance for the long-term unemployed and those who are most disadvantaged in relation to the labour market. There is a danger that services for this group will be under-resourced partly because it is likely that those who have been out of the labour market for longer will require more counselling assistance rather than less, which can prove costly. There is no easy solution to this issue of balancing needs, particularly in times of pressure on resources. Each country will make its own decisions with regard to resource allocations, depending on where priorities are perceived to lie. It is important that in reaching these decisions the perceptions of the different partners are considered as there will be varying viewpoints. These priorities in turn will be affected by factors such as the overall unemployment rates and breakdown of unemployment figures. The approach in countries, such as Ireland, which already have a high percentage of long-term unemployed people, will be different to a country, such as Austria, where more resources are likely to be allocated to preventive work.

Targeted assistance for women

Many women are interested in returning to work but are often not registered as unemployed. This can affect their access to counselling services and other labour market measures as they do not always meet the eligibility criteria because of it. Targeted services for women are required which avoid this eligibility issue and which are locally available, safe, with creche provision and at low cost or free. Examples of this approach can be seen in a number of the Eurocounsel case studies (Appendix 3).

The need for ongoing counselling

Phase 2 has provided some examples of ongoing counselling, or "safety-net" counselling as it was described in the feasibility study for Eurocounsel. This form of provision is particularly targeted at the long-term unemployed and recognises that for some people in this position, re-entry into the labour market or other labour related activities requires ongoing support, if they are not to "drop out" of it. This need for support by some people is about coping with change: there are other measures which can assist in this process such as building up slowly to full-time work starting with one or two days a week, to reduce the impact of the change. However, counselling can play an important role and there is room for further development involving co-operation of employers and trade unions.

A holistic approach to meeting the needs of the long-term unemployed is important

A holistic approach to meeting the needs of the long-term unemployed in particular is important. This recognises that for people who have been out of paid employment for some time that there may be a range of needs to be met including issues of self-confidence or practical problems such as financial debts.

There will be different approaches to meeting these needs. In Austria as has been seen the psychosocial needs are separated out from those relating specifically to labour field opportunities. Another approach advocated at the Eurocounsel conference and linked to the variety of skills which are required of practitioners, is the development of multi-disciplinary teams. This later option has still to be developed fully but offers great potential. The former option is also viable if good networks are in place for ease of referral.

Issues of training of counsellors

Training has continued throughout Phase 2 of Eurocounsel to be one of the areas identified where further improvements can be made. The training needs reflect the complexity of the different kinds of counselling services on offer and the range of practitioners involved. Different existing professions already supply training qualifications and there have been a number of studies in this area undertaken by CEDEFOP, the European Centre for the development of vocational training. (Ref: 20, 21 and 22) Future needs include practical skills in use of new technology as well as the possibility of developing a "labour field counsellor" qualification which merges educational/learning guidance with occupational/labour market counselling. Specialist training, for example, in working with ethnic minorities and immigrants, remains important.

The importance of new technology

Rapid developments are taking place in new technology in relation to counselling and guidance provision. These relate both to the provision of a broad range of information databases and to personality assessments linked to occupational options.
There are a range of software packages which cover a variety of information needs including:

-       occupational information;

-       training and learning opportunities;

-       qualifications;

-       personal profile assessments and psychometric testing.

A research paper prepared for the Third European Conference on Computers in Vocational Guidance held in Nürnberg in November 1992 emphasised the rapid growth that is taking place in this area. (Ref: 16) The author estimated that there are at least 135 different software packages now available in Europe, and countries where the use of computers in guidance had appeared absent a few years earlier, now have research projects underway to develop them: the Spanish Job-Play programme is one example here. The developments of CD-ROM mean that much larger databases can now be held and easily accessed.

The key issues for the future in this area are:

- how to continue to increase the availability and accessibility of information to the user via new technology; will more users be able to access information of this nature in their own homes as the French are able to do via the Minitel system?

- how to integrate the various information software packages which are available (so that if for example, a profile assessment indicates a particular occupation to follow, this can be linked directly to the package which deals with training opportunities, which the user can then access);

- how to manage the growing amounts of information, constantly updating what is available;

- how to relate existing information to local labour market information, (an area which is notoriously weak across Europe) and to increase the Europeanisation of information.

OUTCOMES

Defining Outcomes

There are many ways to define outcomes and these have been outlined in an earlier chapter (pp. 34-38). Outcomes relate both to issues of personal development as well as to awareness of all the opportunities available and the ability to take decisions leading to specific action. The outcomes desired may vary between the user, the counselling practitioner and the agency providing the service.

Methods for measurement

The key issue in relation to the outcomes of counselling is for the further development of methods to measure quality and performance. There are a number of important issues to consider concerning the kinds of measurement used (quantitative or qualitative) when measurements are taken and who decides what is quality. The Irish consultants in their report (Ref: 10) have examined these issues in some detail. It is true to say that quantitative measurements still outweigh qualitative ones but even here there are problems concerning access to information about those who are registered as unemployed and time constraints in undertaking methods such as tracking studies. The importance of involving users themselves in assessment of services has been highlighted and user surveys are now undertaken, for example, by the public employment services in some countries, such as Denmark and the UK.

There are also questions as to what is measured: is it the quality of the process itself or only the identifiable outcomes. This latter area raises its own issues as not all outcomes are immediately tangible even though the process has been a positive one and has had benefits for the individual concerned. Further research and clear exposition of the findings are required so that this important area can be advanced.

Linked to the methods for measurement and evaluation is the broader need to make the case for counselling. This is particularly important at a time of limited resources so that policy makers can be clear as to the importance of this service provision. Making the case for counselling should be based not only on its economic value but also its social one: the ways in which counselling can assist in the reduction of social exclusion is as important as its direct economic value to the labour market.

RECOMMENDATIONS

Based on the findings of Phase 2, 15 key recommendations are made below. It is recognised that there are many further ways to improve services, often by action at local level and by individual organisations and practitioners However, these 14 recommendations cover the main results from this second phase of Eurocounsel.

1. A decentralised approach to the provision of counselling

With increasing decentralisation in most European countries there is already a move towards a decentralised approach to the provision of counselling which should be encouraged. Such an approach allows for the development of a comprehensive model of counselling adapted to the needs of the particular local labour market situation. Central governments should be responsible for the provision of overall guidelines and financial resources but allow each area to tailor provision according to its needs in terms of the labour market, population make-up and the providers involved.

This recommendation is seen as of top priority as it will facilitate several of the recommendations which are to follow here.

2.   **The development of multi-disciplinary teams as well as specialist targeted services.**

In order to meet a wide range of the users' needs and avoiding as much as possible the referral of users to several different agencies, it will be practical to develop within each area some general multi-disciplinary teams of staff who between them cover the range of skills required to offer effective counselling to the whole potential client group, both those currently in employment and those who are unemployed. However alongside this it will be important to continue with some specialist targeted services which will be more accessible to those whom they are intended to serve. Specialist services are particularly important for those who might otherwise be excluded, such as some women, ethnic minorities and immigrants, or those with specialist needs such as people with disabilities.

3.   **Greater involvement of the users**

Phase 2 has given clear indications that more user involvement in the design and evaluation of services is desirable. Such involvement increases the chances that services will meet the users' needs effectively and allows a mechanism for continual improvements to the services to be made through the practitioners providing feedback to policy makers and providers about users' perceptions. It also increases users' confidence in those services and the sense that their needs will be met. There needs to be further examination of the practical ways in which this can be achieved.

4.   **Support for self-help initiatives**

Linked to increasing user involvement is the need to promote ways to support self-help initiatives. These will often involve counselling practitioners in a different role to that of the counsellor-client one and it is likely that those involved in this area will have specific training needs. Other resources required for such initiatives may include premises and equipment.

5.   **Counselling services for all adults**

Although recognising the constraints in terms of resources, one of the recommendations to improve services is to examine ways to make them available to all adults of working age. It is believed that in this way each country is more likely to benefit from the full potential of its labour force. Counselling and guidance can help people to find the most appropriate routes for their abilities in relation to available opportunities and will ease and encourage labour market transitions and rotations. At the same time, targeted services for those who are long-term unemployed will be needed particularly as even when unemployment begins to decrease again, a significantly greater number of people than previously will remain long-term unemployed, unless action is taken. OECD's work has clearly pointed to this 'rachet' effect.

6. Training for practitioners

Both in the feasibility work for the Eurocounsel programme and in the Phase 1 report, the issue of training for practitioners was raised. During Phase 2 this issue has been given attention in many countries as well as at European level by bodies such as CEDEFOP (Ref: 9) and this must be encouraged to continue. There are a number of areas where practitioners themselves recognize the need for training. These include:

- in the use of new technology;

- in support for self-help initiatives;

- in understanding of the different functions of counselling.

7. Continuation of study visit programme

The pilot study visit programme undertaken as part of the work of Phase 2 of Eurocounsel has provided a form of training for those who participated and has had clear benefits. These benefits include the transfer of practical experience and the opportunity to exchange ideas and develop new networks. It has enhanced the European dimension of counselling. It is recommended that ways to continue such study visits for practitioners are investigated and funding sought.

8. Encourage early intervention and prevention

It has been shown that major industries have recognised the importance of early intervention in preventing long-term unemployment. Such early intervention should be encouraged, particularly in small and medium sized enterprises facing redundancies.

9. Increasing understanding of the "activating" function of counselling

The "activating" function of counselling is linked to the need to understand the full range of opportunities for labour, particularly in areas where there is low demand for it in the primary labour market. Counsellors will require understanding of all of these opportunities. Particularly important will be the need to understand the routes into self-employment and employment creation.

10. Continuing development of counselling methods

There should continue to be development of counselling methods. Personal action planning, group counselling and other methods should be encouraged. There is a need to examine interventions which use practical and semi-practical methods and not just talking along with a range of ways in which the user can access services for themselves. As in any profession there is a need constantly to refine and improve on methods and techniques.

11. New technology

New technology is part of the future of counselling provision. It is one important element in improvements to the development and management of information provision within counselling. Much has already been developed in some European countries and this information needs to be readily available to other countries which are just beginning to make increased use of new technology within their counselling services. It is also important to review ways in which other countries e.g. the USA and Canada may be ahead of Europe in this field. In both cases this will avoid duplication of effort.

The training needs of counselling practitioners in relation to new technology need to be addressed as mentioned in the section above on training.

12. Methods for measurement

The need to refine methods for measurement of quality and performance in counselling services has been raised in both Phases 1 and 2 of Eurocounsel. A research review of the work already undertaken in this area would be helpful followed by the production of a practical guide for counselling services in a range of different kinds of organisation as to how to undertake measurement and evaluation.

13.   The development of local and transnational networks

One of the most important recommendations to emerge from Phase 2 of Eurocounsel concerns the promotion of networks both at regional level and transnationally. At local level networking will be assisted by the regional approach to counselling provision described above. Formal as well as informal networks are needed to best meet the needs of the users, and to avoid wastage of resources. Users should have representation on these networks wherever possible.

At transnational level there has been a specific request, from delegates at the Eurocounsel conference in Dublin, to establish a European network of practitioners, policy makers and researchers in this area. Ways to take this suggestion forward should be examined.

14.   The role of the social partners

Employers should be encouraged to continue closer involvement with the providers of counselling services in particular the public employment services. This will allow counselling practitioners to offer more informed advice and will enable the needs of the labour market to be more accurately met. Such closer links will also help to improve the negative perceptions which many employers hold of the long-term unemployed and make it more likely for them to be considered as recruits.

If a comprehensive counselling service is provided to all adults, for those in employment as well as job seekers, this will have implications for employers. This is already recognised by some employers who make provision within training and learning budgets to give employees time for such counselling assistance. It is seen as part of being a "learning company" which is a growing trend in many countries.

The trade unions can play an important role in promoting the need for preventive counselling (which has already begun to happen). It will also be important for them to consider other ways in which they can support their members to obtain assistance with counselling and guidance. Phase 2 has provided examples of trade union training for shop stewards so that they can themselves offer counselling in this area. The trade unions also play an important role in relation to the unemployed, for example, through providing financial resources for unemployed workers' centres.

Both employers and trade union organisations can also contribute to the further development of counselling provision through involvement in networks, partnerships and lobbying and through the European social dialogue.

15.   A European focus

It is one thing to identify the ways to improve counselling services but there are problems associated with introducing new areas and changes to existing systems and structures. The ideas of partnerships, self-help initiatives or neutral provision may not fit in easily to the existing culture. This point lends even greater weight to the importance of a European focus and networking so that such barriers can be tackled and people can have the chance to see ideas and practices in place where they are working successfully. This greater European focus should include improved co-ordination of all the work being undertaken at European level on issues relating to labour field counselling.

6   PROSPECTS FOR THE FUTURE

The preceding chapters have described the results of the second phase of Eurocounsel and have provided recommendations as to ways in which services can be improved. It will not be possible nor appropriate for all of these recommendations to be taken forward by the Eurocounsel programme: some of them will be advanced by other organisations, at European, national and local levels. This chapter examines some of the practical ways in which the recommendations can be taken forward, both by a third phase of the Eurocounsel programme and by other means.

Suggestions for Phase 3 from the local consultants' reports.

The local consultants have made a range of suggestions for further work in this area which include the following:

-       investigating ways to measure quality and evaluate services;

-       research into the benefits and drawbacks of including transnational elements in counselling activities for the long-term unemployed;

-       the need to investigate the economic and social value of counselling;

-       issues of counselling linked to environmental development;

-       counselling services to support the unemployed in business development;

-       new counselling techniques for practitioners working with low-skilled clients;

-       development of a methodology that would allow for up-to-date knowledge of the local labour market;

-       further analysis of the role of counselling services in relation to varying institutional and cultural characteristics and labour market measures;

-       counselling provision for immigrants in European countries;

-       counselling activities within other European programmes, such as LEADER, the rural development programme;

- ways to include users in the design of services;

- the development of a regional model of co-operation;

- further development of criteria of efficiency and effectiveness.

Research suggestions for Phase 3 of Eurocounsel

Having considered these, it is suggested that the third phase of Eurocounsel should focus on in-depth research work to take forward some of the ideas which have emerged during Phase 2. A lot has been gained during this phase in the three meetings of local consultants and it is proposed that further opportunities for the local consultants to work in this way, allowing for an exchange of ideas and findings, would be beneficial.

The key issues which appear to require further investigation are as follows:

- counselling linked to the creation of new opportunities: how can counselling best play a role in local economic development and the creation of new employment and other opportunities? This is an area which is of particular importance in the current context of rising unemployment in Europe which looks set to continue over the next year. At national and European levels new measures are being investigated to promote employment growth, and counselling has a key role to play in relation to these measures. The research issues to be examined include a focus on counselling needs and existing practice in relation to self-employment, as well as on the counselling support needed to establish other forms of labour related activities;

- what is existing practice across Europe with regard to measuring the quality and effectiveness of services and how do countries differ in their approach to this issue? This is a subject area which has arisen continually during Phase 2 of Eurocounsel. It is connected to the question of resource limitations and the need to use available resources in the most effective manner possible. It also relates to the need to make the case for counselling to policy makers. The results of such work will therefore affect counselling provision at different levels: the counselling services themselves and policy making in this area. One practical output from this research would be to develop guidelines to enable more services to measure and evaluate what they offer and use the results to make improvements. These guidelines should include ways to involve users in the measurement and evaluation procedures;

- the role of partnerships, intermediaries and alternative delivery structures in counselling provision. It is important to investigate these structures further because as the labour market, and labour related activities become both more dynamic and complex, so too do the counselling structures needed to support them. This research will assist in the understanding of new developments in this area, highlighting successful models and examining differences between approaches in different countries.

A study visits programme

The pilot study visit programme undertaken in Phase 2 of Eurocounsel had a number of useful benefits including the opportunity for participating practitioners to reflect on their own practice through learning about another country's approach to counselling provision at first hand. It is seen as a method of training and many of those who took part have suggested that further such programmes be mounted.

It will be useful to investigate ways in which further study visits could be organised. This might be linked to the creation of a new European network for labour related counselling discussed below.

The establishment of a European network

The Eurocounsel conference in Dublin produced a strong demand for the creation of a European network for all those connected to this area of labour related counselling. Such a network might for example allow for the continuation of the exchange of ideas and practices through the holding of transnational seminars. This was one of the outcomes of the conference which participants particularly welcomed and wanted to see continued. It is suggested that one of the practical ways to take forward this idea will be to hold a preliminary meeting of key interested people to plan what is wanted. This meeting could perhaps be funded by the Foundation or by another European organisation.

One of the ways forward on this will be to examine how other networks have been established, are funded and operate. In particular it is suggested that a review of the way in which the European Group of Local Employment Initiatives (EGLEI) was formed (including organisation of study tours), will provide a useful starting point and there will be other networks which can be similarly examined. It is important to take at least this preliminary action on what was one of the key recommendations of the Eurocounsel conference.

Further research areas

New technology

There are a whole range of research needs relating to the developments in new technology, and it is recognised that there are specialist researchers in this area who may already be investigating some of them. These needs include ways to increase the availability of information directly to users, and ways to relate existing information databases to local labour market information (an issue which is commented upon further in the next paragraph). It is suggested that it may be useful to undertake a review of innovative developments concerning the use of new technology in this area both within the European Community and outside it. Funding to undertake such research will be required.

Local labour market information

This is an area which is mentioned as a weakness in many reports about general economic development and it is one which needs to be addressed. Practical and appropriate ways to gather information on a regular basis and to disseminate it to those who will make use of it are required. This is an essential piece of research which perhaps could best be tackled at European level so that the information from a series of local labour markets could be contrasted and linked in to the EURES programme.

A European approach would also allow for a comparison of different methods of collecting and disseminating local labour market information to be made. It is important that this should go beyond a statistical approach only and include ways to add qualitative information as it is this kind of information that is often of most use to counselling practitioners.

Training

CEDEFOP, the European Centre for the Development of Vocational Training, is well placed to take further suggestions about the training needs of counselling practitioners and has already undertaken several studies in this area. (Ref: 20-23)

Relating developments in public employment services to general public service developments

It will be useful to undertake research which links developments in public employment services in several countries to general public service developments. The Foundation has already been involved in this aspect of work, investigating user involvement in services and consumer oriented actions. Linkages between these two areas may prove fruitful.

Conclusion

Phase 2 of Eurocounsel has been a productive one and has highlighted the areas in which counselling services can begin to be improved. The importance of counselling at a time of ever rising unemployment has been emphasized and has led to a sharper focus on the roles which counselling has to play in relation to the broad range of labour related activities. There is a need for the Foundation to continue to contribute in this important work through a further phase of Eurocounsel. This will allow networks and expertise to be developed, in-depth research on the issues highlighted to be undertaken and for all the findings to be widely disseminated through a variety of methods including publications and presentations. Eurocounsel to date has helped to focus greater attention on counselling services in relation to the prevention and solution of long-term unemployment and it is important to build on what has been achieved so far.

REFERENCES

1. Counselling and Long-term Unemployment: Report on Phase 1 of the Eurocounsel Action Research Programme, Luxembourg: Office for Official Publications of the European Communities, 1992. (available in EN, FR, DE, IT, ES, DA)

2. Counselling and Long-term Unemployment: Report on Phase 1 of the Eurocounsel Action Research Programme. Executive Summary, Dublin; European Foundation for the Improvement of Living and Working Conditions, 1992. (available in all EC working languages)

3. Counselling for the Unemployed: Issues for Policy Makers, Dublin: European Foundation for the Improvement of Living and Working Conditions, 1991. (EFILWC Working Paper: available in all EC working languages)

4. Counselling for the Unemployed: Issues for Practitioners, Dublin: European Foundation for the Improvement of Living and Working Conditions, 1991. (EFILWC Working Paper: available in all EC working languages)

5. Seminar for Senior Public Employment Service Officials: Edinburgh, 25-27 January, 1993. European Foundation for the Improvement of Living and Working Conditions, 1993. [EFILWC Working Paper].

6. Eurocounsel Conference held in Dublin 24-26 May 1993: Improving Counselling Services for those who are unemployed or at risk of becoming so. Publication of report (to be published). European Foundation for the Improvement of Living and Working Conditions, 1993.

7. Eurocounsel Case Study Portfolio: Examples of Innovative Practice in Labour Market Counselling. European Foundation for the Improvement of Living and Working Conditions, 1993. (to be published).

8. Austria: Final Report of Eurocounsel Phase 2, by Petra Draxl. ÖSB Unternehmensberatung, Vienna, 1993. (Available in English and German).

9. Denmark: Eurocounsel Phase 2 Final Report, by Peter Plant. European Foundation for the Improvement of Living and Working Conditions, 1993. (Available in English and Danish).

10. Germany: Counselling and long-term unemployment: Eurocounsel - Phase 2 Final Report for Germany, by Jürgen Schumacher and Karin Stiehr. European Foundation for the Improvement of Living and Working Conditions, 1993. (Available in English and German).

11. Ireland: Eurocounsel Phase 2 Final Report, by Carmel Duggan and Tom Ronayne. European Foundation for the Improvement of Living and Working Conditions, 1993. (Available in English).

12. Italy: Eurocounsel Phase 2 Final Report, by Gianni Geroldi and Marco Maeillo. European Foundation for the Improvement of Living and Working Conditions, 1993. (Available in English and Italian).

13. Spain: Eurocounsel - Final Report of Phase 2, by Lina Gavira and Francisco Gonzales. European Foundation for the Improvement of Living and Working Conditions, 1993. (Available in English and Spanish).

14. United Kingdom: Eurocounsel Phase 2 Final Report by Rita Griffiths. European Foundation for the Improvement of Living and Working Conditions, 1993. (Available in English).

15. Education, Unemployment and Future of Work, by A.G. Watts, Milton Keynes Open University Press, 1983.

16. Developments in the field of vocational guidance software: paper by Marcus Offer, Third European Conference on computers in Careers guidance, Nürnberg, 1992.

17. Employment Framework: Commission of the European Communities, Brussels 1993.

18. Educational and Vocational guidance in the European Community: Synthesis Report: Commission of the European Communities, Brussels, 1993.

19. European Handbook for Guidance Counsellors/PETRA-Task Force Human Resources, Education, Training, Youth. Commission of the European Communities - Bad Honnef: Bock, 1993 (available in EN, FR, DE)

20. Vocational guidance and counselling for adults. Summary report on the services available for the unemployed and especially the long-term unemployed. CEDEFOP, 1990. (available in DE, EN, FR), Luxembourg: Office for Official Publications of the European Communities.

21. Transnational vocational guidance and training for young people and adults, CEDEFOP, 1990. (available in DE, EN, FR). Luxembourg: Office for Official Publications of the European Communities.

22. Transnational vocational guidance and training for young people and adults. Synthesis report of eight studies, CEDEFOP, 1990. (available in DE, EN, FR). Luxembourg: Office for Official Publications of the European Communities.

23. Occupational profiles of vocational counsellors in the European Community: A synthesis report. Luxembourg: Office for Official Publications of the European Communities, 1992.

24.   ERGO Final Report Phase I: Commission of the European Communities, Brussels, 1992.

25.   Council Resolution on Vocational Education and Training in the 1990s: Official Journal of the European Communities, C186, July 8th 1993.

EUROCOUNSEL ADVISORY COMMITTEE AND LOCAL CONSULTANTS

ADVISORY COMMITTEE

Representative of
TRADE UNION GROUP

Mr. Paolo Adurno
ETUC
European Trade Union Confederation
Boulevard Emile Jacqumain 155
B-1210 Brussels
Belgium
Tel: +32 2 2240419
Fax: +32 2 2240454/55

Representatives of
EMPLOYERS GROUP

Mr. Xenophon Constantinidis
Association interentreprise pour la
Formation professionelle et industrielle
24 Karolou St.
Gr-10437 Athens
Greece
Tel: +30-1-52.32.088
Fax: +30-1-52.30.344

Mr. Bernard Le Marchand
Avenue Victor Gilsoul 76
B-1200 Brussels
Belgium
Tel: +32-2-771.58.71
Fax: +32-2-771.58.71

Representative of
GOVERNMENT GROUP

Dr. Stanley King
International Relations Branch
Department of Employment
Room 607
Steel House
Tothill Street
London SW1H 9NF
U.K.
Tel: +44-71-273.51.38
Fax: +44-71-273.56.11/273.59.88

Representative of
Commission of the EC

Mr. Danny Brennan
Commission of the EC, DG V
Rue de la Loi, 200
B-1049 Brussels
Belgium
Tel: +32-2-295.42.72
Fax: +32-2-295.65.07

Representative of OECD	Mr. Donald McBain OECD 2, rue André-Pascal F-75775 Paris Cedex 16 France Tel: +33-1-45.24.91.63 Fax: +33-1-45.24.90.98
Representative of ILO	Mr. Sergio Ricca ILO Labour Administration Branch P.O. Box 500 CH-1211 Geneva 22 Switzerland Tel: +41-22-799.70.49 Fax: +41-22-798.86.85
Representative of Committee of Experts	Mr. Bill Daniel Flat 3 Rotherwood 8 Maer Down Road Bude North Cornwall EX23 8QU U.K. Tel: +44-288-356.678
Representative of CEDEFOP	Ms. Gesa Chomé CEDEFOP Bundesallee 22 D-10717 Berlin Federal Republic of Germany Tel: +49-30-88-41.21.64 Fax: +49-30-88.41.22.22

EUROCOUNSEL LOCAL CONSULTANTS

AUSTRIA

Petra Draxl
ÖSB Unternehmensberatung GmbH
Neubaugasse 31
A-1070 Vienna
Tel: +43-222-93 15 38
Fax: +43-222-93 33 29

DENMARK

Peter Plant
Margrethevej 3
DK-2960 Rungsted Kyst
Tel: +45-39-69 66 33
Fax: +45-39-69 74 74

GERMANY

Karin Stiehr and Jürgen Schumacher
INBAS
Kaiserstraße 61
D-60329 Frankfurt/Main 1
Tel: +49-69-252 922
Fax: +49-69-252 777

IRELAND

Tom Ronayne and Carmel Duggan
WRC Social and Economic Consultants Ltd
4 Lower Ormond Quay
Dublin 1
Tel: +353-1-872 31 00
Fax: +353-1-872 38 40

ITALY

Marco Maiello and Gianni Geroldi
Fondazione Seveso
Viale Tunisia 2
I-20124 Milan
Tel: +39-2-29-52 32 37
Fax: +39-2-29-51 89 71

SPAIN

Lina Gavira and Francisco Gonzalez
c/o Departamento de Sociologia
Facultad de Ciencias Economicas
y Empresariales
Universidad de Sevilla
Av. Ramon y Cajal s/n
41005 Sevilla
Tel: +34-5-441 02 46
Fax: +34-5-455 13 84

UNITED KINGDOM

Rita Griffiths
The Planning Exchange
3 Worsley Road
Worsley
Manchester M28 4NN
Tel: +44-61-727 8677
Fax: +44-61-727 8675

PROGRAMME
CO-ORDINATORS

Glenys Watt, Norma Hurley and Pamela Reid
Blake Stevenson Ltd
12/A Cumberland Street
South East Lane
Edinburgh EH3 6RU
Tel: +44-31-558 30 01
Fax: +44-31-556 34 22

Appendix 2

IMPROVING COUNSELLING SERVICES FOR THOSE
WHO ARE UNEMPLOYED OR AT RISK OF BECOMING SO

The Eurocounsel Conference

Dublin, 24-26 May 1993

WORKING PAPER FOR INTRODUCTORY WORKSHOP

**European Foundation
for the Improvement
of Living and
Working Conditions**

Loughlinstown House
Shankill
Co. Dublin
Ireland
Tel: (Int+353)1 2826888
Fax: (Int+353)1 2826456
  or (Int+353)1 2824209
Telex: 30726 EURF EI
Email postmaster@eurofound.ie

EUROPÄISCHE STIFTUNG ZUR VERBESSERUNG DER LEBENS- UND ARBEITSBEDINGUNGEN
FONDATION EUROPÉENNE POUR L'AMÉLIORATION DES CONDITIONS DE VIE ET DE TRAVAIL
EUROPESE STICHTING TOT VERBETERING VAN DE LEVENS- EN ARBEIDSOMSTANDIGHEDEN
ΕΥΡΩΠΑΪΚΟ ΙΔΡΥΜΑ ΓΙΑ ΤΗΝ ΒΕΛΤΙΩΣΗ ΤΩΝ ΣΥΝΘΗΚΩΝ ΔΙΑΒΙΩΣΕΩΣ ΚΑΙ ΕΡΓΑΣΙΑΣ

DET EUROPÆISKE INSTITUT TIL FORBEDRING AF LEVE- OG ARBEJDSVILKÅRENE
FUNDAÇÃO EUROPEIA PARA A MELHORIA DAS CONDIÇÕES DE VIDA E DE TRABALHO
FUNDACIÓN EUROPEA PARA LA MEJORA DE LAS CONDICIONES DE VIDA Y DE TRABAJO
FONDAZIONE EUROPEA PER IL MIGLIORAMENTO DELLE CONDIZIONI DI VITA E DI LAVORO

1 COUNSELLING SERVICES AND LONG-TERM UNEMPLOYMENT: IDENTIFYING GAPS AND SETTING PRIORITIES

Introduction

1.1 This short paper serves as an introduction to the first workshop session at the Eurocounsel conference to be held in Dublin in May. It is intended that it should be read in conjunction with the Executive Summary for Phase 1 of Eurocounsel which has been sent to all conference participants with the invitation to attend.

1.2 The aim of the Eurocounsel programme is to improve counselling services for the unemployed and those at risk of becoming so. One important approach to improving services is to identify where the gaps currently are and what the priorities should be for meeting the identified needs.

1.3 The findings of Eurocounsel to date have shown clearly that there are a wide range of counselling services throughout Europe in the public, private and voluntary sectors. The kinds of services offered and the ways in which they are provided vary from country to country and also within each country (See Phase 1 Executive Summary). The variety of service provision means that the gaps, needs and priorities also vary. Even within one regional area, individuals concerned with the provision of counselling services will hold different views as to what the key issues are and how best to improve the services offered. The purpose of the first workshop is to allow participants to air their views about the key gaps and the priorities for improving services.

1.4 The purpose of this paper is to stimulate your thinking about what would be the best ways to improve counselling services in your region/country in advance of the conference itself. We recognise of course that counselling services cannot solve all the problems of rapidly rising unemployment, and that there is a pressing need for new and creative macro employment policies to address this issue. However, our focus is on counselling services and the role they can play. We hope that participants will come to the first workshop of the Eurocounsel conference having thought carefully about what they perceive to be the main gaps in services and the top priorities for tackling these groups. We have given a table of gaps in Section 3 which we would ask you to fill in, adding to the gaps and identifying the priorities in your area/country. Please bring your filled in sheet to the conference. We expect to have some lively discussion about our different views on this at the first workshop session.

1.5 In writing this paper we have had to make some generalisations. Not all the gaps we describe are found throughout Europe. Each country is at a different stage in its development of counselling services and has a different economic and political context in which to set them. However the findings of Eurocounsel to date demonstrate that there are some common gaps and that people have already begun to identify what some of the priorities might be. We have not attempted to list all the gaps which might be found, but those which seem particularly striking.

1.6 The paper is set out in the following way:

-      firstly, the gaps are analysed according to the customers/clients; the providers; the content of what is provided; and issues to do with how and when the services are provided as well as research gaps;

-      secondly, the identified gaps are summarised in a table and we ask you to add the gaps you have perceived in your own country in the spaces provided.

2   THE GAPS

2.1   As set out in the Executive Summary the definition of counselling that we are using throughout the Eurocounsel programme is that it includes services which involve the following:

-    information provision;

-    advice;

-    guidance;

-    counselling.

2.2   The gaps in services are described in this section under the four headings shown below:

-    customers/ clients;

-    providers;

-    content/ methods;

-    general issues.

Customers/clients

2.3   Many of the counselling services provided throughout Europe regard the unemployed whom they help as clients rather than customers. In other words the power in the relationship tends to be one way. This is in some ways not surprising as many public sector counselling services are linked to a person's benefits payments and there is an element of compulsion involved. Where the provision of services is kept separate from the provision of unemployment benefits, then this balance of power is likely to be more equal.

2.4   Most of the counselling services target the unemployed people as a homogeneous group. One of the gaps therefore is in targeting and tailoring services to specific segments of the unemployed population: male/female; young/older people; people with special needs (ex-offenders/people with disability/minority groups).

2.5   Even where specific groups of people are targeted, there is often stereotyping and not enough focus on the individual person's needs.

2.6   Similarly there are gaps in who is eligible for counselling services and at what stage. Early intervention is seen by many as helping to reduce the number of those who go on to become long-term unemployed, but counselling is expensive and is often only available when a serious problem of unemployment already exists.

2.7   This leads to the question of whether counselling should be made more widely available to everyone who finds themselves in a period of transition in relation to the labour market. Such transition periods might include people who want to move from one job to another, people who are coming up to retirement or people who want to reassess their long-term aims. This move to provide counselling and vocational guidance services to all adults on request has already begun in some countries.

Providers

2.8   The majority of providers of counselling come under state provision and work in public sector organisations. These may come under the auspices of ministries of labour or ministries of education. In some countries there is also a non- government sector providing such services. In general there is a wide diversity of providers and the key issue for the consumer is whether this is a good thing or not. It may, on the one hand, be helpful to have diversity in terms of choice, but on the other hand people may not find the best service to suit their needs or may find the plethora of services confusing.

2.9   Key gaps identified by providers during the Eurocounsel programme to date include the following:

-    the need for training and a qualification structure which is targeted at providers of counselling services in relation to the labour market;

-    linked to the above, the need for recognition and status as a profession;

-    the importance of local, regional and national networking structures so that providers from the different institutions know each other and what services they each have to offer; for example, being able to refer someone with ease and confidence to an agency providing information about job opportunities across Europe (see 2.15);

-    the need for identification of good practice and examples of how to improve services aimed at practitioners.

2.10   There is counselling provision in some countries for employees in large companies which are facing massive redundancies. However it is more rare to find counselling services provided in small and medium sized companies which know they are about to lay people off and this is one area in which there is room for more provision. This kind of preventative counselling is likely to be one of the main areas for further development in the future.

2.11   Another gap is the need in some countries for a greater number of trained providers to be able to offer more by way of counselling services. This is affected by the political context of the country in which the services are placed. In some countries the ratio of clients to counsellors means that in practice either not all the clients will receive a service or if they all do then that service will be minimal.

Content

What is provided?

2.12   Information is the most commonly found element within counselling services which have been researched during Eurocounsel. In most countries there is room to develop more services which focus on the empowerment of the individual, that is they are concerned with "counselling" in its purest sense.

2.13   However even in terms of information provision it appears that practitioners often lack up to date and precise information about the local labour market, about the services which other local agencies are supplying and about career choice in general.

2.14 In relation to the functions of counselling there is a need to explore what services can most usefully be offered to those in situations where there are no or few existing jobs in the labour market. This may involve counselling to create new employment initiatives of various kinds as well as assisting people to find other activities (perhaps in the form of voluntary work or new hobbies) which keep them motivated.

2.15 An increasingly important issue, if there are few jobs locally, is to be able to provide information and advice about opportunities throughout EC countries, or at least to know which agency will be able to do this.

2.16 One to one provision is the commonest form in which services are provided. There is space to explore other methods of provision in particular group methods. These have been seen to be effective in a number of counselling situations not related to the labour market, partly because they involve peers within a similar situation assisting each other.

How is it provided

2.17 The most appropriate methods to meet the needs of the individual have to be addressed. For example, new technology can play a useful role in information provision, leaving the counselling practitioners with more time in which to offer in-depth counselling, advice and guidance.

2.18 Most services are provided in centrally based offices in cities and towns. There is much that can be done (again thinking of the person using the service as customer rather than client) to make services more accessible. Issues of access which need to be considered range from privacy during the counselling session, to the general image presented, to outreach services.

Research

2.19 Measuring the quality of the services which are offered is one area which needs to be improved in most instances. Research will be needed to draw up a model of how such measurement can be done and what criteria should be used.

2.20 Similarly, to assist in making the case for greater resources (to employ more practitioners and provide more services) there is a need for research to examine fully the cost-benefits of the provision of counselling services. Politicians and policy makers require some hard evidence that money spent on such services is producing results.

2.21 Research is also needed to examine whether some groups within the unemployed, benefit more from the assistance of counselling services than others; whether compulsion is of benefit or not and whether there are particular times when it is more useful to provide services. For example in some countries, no services are provided for the first three months as it is believed that during this time many people will find their way back into the labour market quite quickly and that those who are still unemployed at the end of that time are the people who most need assistance. The results from such research would be particularly useful where resources are scarce and assistance needs to be targeted in the most effective ways.

Creative gaps

2.22 There are a number of general gaps which may not be about what is missing as such but may be about the need to be creative in improving services. For example, it might be helpful to envisage counselling services in relation to the labour market and to individual development which are available throughout a person's working life and which both those in work at present and those who are not can make use of. This would lead to the development of an integrated counselling service which starts when an individual is still at school and which continues to their retirement. There are probably many more examples which participants who attend the conference can contribute.

3 **SETTING PRIORITIES**

3.1 In the matrix on the next page we have summarised the gaps identified in Section 2 and left space for you to add your own.

3.2 We have then entitled the second column, "Priorities" and would ask you to tick those of the gaps which you think to be most urgently in need of action. The third column is called "Action" and in this we ask you to write down the action you think appropriate for the Priorities you have ticked.

PLEASE BRING THIS WITH YOU TO THE CONFERENCE!

THE GAPS	PRIORITY?	SUGGESTED ACTION
Customers/Clients 1 The need to balance the power relationship between user and provider.		
2 The need (where appropriate) to separate provision of benefits from provision of counselling.		
3 The need to tailor services to different target groups.		
4 "Individualising" service provision.		
5 Provision of counselling services as early intervention.		
6 Counselling services for all those facing working life transitions		
7 *Other?*		

THE GAPS	PRIORITY?	SUGGESTED ACTION
Providers 1 The need for training and a qualification structure 2 Recognition of the profession 3 Examples of good practice 4 <u>More</u> providers! 5 Wider provision of services for those whose employment is at risk. 6 The need for more networks and referral between providers 7 *Other?*		

THE GAPS	PRIORITY	SUGGESTED ACTION
Content 1 Development of role of counselling to empower the individual		
2 The need for more up-to-date labour market information		
3 Development of choice of routes in areas where there are few existing jobs		
4 Explore new methods, in particular greater use of group counselling		
5 Improve access to services		
6 *Other?*		

THE GAPS	PRIORITY	SUGGESTED ACTION
Research 1 Development of a model for measuring the quality of counselling services 2 Research into the cost benefits of provision of counselling 3 Research into the effectiveness of: - targeting specific groups/individuals; - offering services at specific times; - whether compulsion is helpful. "Creative Gaps" 4 Development of a fully integrated service for the whole of an individual's active working life 5 *Other?*		

LIST OF CASE STUDIES:

COUNSELLING EMPHASIS:

Titles	Preventive/solving/ coping	Page No.
Austria		
Counselling Centre for Young Women and Girls	Preventive/Solving	7
Work/Labour Foundations in the Aluminium and Steel Industries	Preventive	11
Counselling and Help for Psychosocially Disadvantaged Persons	Preventive/Solving	15
Denmark		
Self-governing Counselling in Maribo	Preventive/Coping	19
Outreach Counselling for Young People in Holbaek	Preventive/Solving	22
Unions in Action: Counselling in the Workplace	Preventive	24
Germany		
A joint/combined project approach to counselling participants entering Employment Schemes in Saarland	Preventive/Solving	28
Support for self-motivated information seeking in Thüringen	Solving/Coping	30
Women Returners: Career Planning Guidelines in Saarbrücken	Solving	33
Ireland		
Building Guidance into a Work Experience Programme in Tallaght	Solving	37
Guidance and Counselling to Women: Parenting Alone	Solving	40
Developmental Intervention for the Unemployed	Coping	42

STANDARD FORMAT OF CASE STUDIES ON COUNSELLING PRACTICES

*   Title of Case Study

*   Name, Address and Contact Name for Project

*   Languages Spoken

*   Initial Description of the Project - the context

*   The Innovative Practice - the content

*   Analysis

*   Potential Lessons

EUROCOUNSEL: SAMPLE CASE STUDY

GREENVALE OPPORTUNITIES SHOP
30 GREENVALE ROAD
GREENVALE

Tel: 091 555 3456

Fax: 091 334 5678

Contact Name: Hamish McFarlane, Manager

Languages spoken: Staff speak English and French

1   THE CONTEXT: INTRODUCTION AND INITIAL DESCRIPTION

1.1   Greenvale Opportunities Shop is a community-based service offering counselling and advice on education and training opportunities to employed and unemployed people over sixteen years of age. The Shop is situated in a housing estate on the outskirts of one of the major Scottish cities.

1.2   The Shop was established in 1989 to address the problems of low skills and high unemployment in the area. It is run by a Management Committee comprised of local residents and is staffed by ten professional workers appointed by the Committee.

1.3   The Shop is funded by a mixture of sources including the Economic Development Committee of the local authority, the European Social Fund, and the Local Enterprise Company. The policy and management of the Shop is in the hands of the Committee and the Shop is run as an independent charitable organisation.

2   THE CONTENT: THE INNOVATIVE PRACTICE IN GREENVALE OPPORTUNITIES SHOP

Access

2.1   The Greenvale Opportunities Shop provides a variety of counselling services. Access is open to anyone, without an appointment, and the shop is physically accessible to people in wheelchairs and parents with children in buggies. There is a creche where young children can be cared for whilst their parents are attending interviews or courses. All services are free and confidential.

Services Provided

2.2   Counselling services are comprehensive and range from front line information and advice about education and training courses through to indepth individual guidance. The range of services includes:

*   basic information on education and training courses, available from picking up leaflets, browsing through reference material, or from a reception worker;

*   individual interviews with a professional guidance counsellor;

*   access to a computerised database listing all the educational and training courses available in the locality;

*   vocational and personal guidance courses of varying duration, some targeted on special needs groups, e.g. women returners. people with disabilities;

*   access to computer assisted analysis of vocational aptitudes and interests.

Counselling philosophy and practice

2.3   The basic philosophy of the counselling service is that it responds to customers needs and is totally individualised. There is no set formula for "Counselling" for all customers, nor is there a set period of time allotted to each customer.

The Users View of the Services

2.4   The users of the service like the informality of the approach, the confidentiality, the independence of the policy and management of the shop, especially that it has no direct links with government employment or welfare agencies, the quality of the guidance offered, and the support services provided, such as the creche.

Strengths of the Shops Counselling services

2.5   The independence of the Shop, its commitment to high quality counselling, its flexibility of approach, and its friendly informality are among the strengths of its counselling services.

Weakness of the Shop

2.6   The Shop has one major weakness in that it does not follow up its customers on a regular and systematic basis and therefore has little real sense of how successful its counselling services have been in the longer term, i.e. over a period of a year or two.

3   **ANALYSIS**

3.1   The following factors make this shop of interest:

* it is run and managed by local people;
* it is flexible and responsive
* it is centred on the needs of the customer and working with the customer to explore options and choices in education and training;
* it values customers' experiences and potential, rather than seeing them as lacking in aptitude or ability.

3.2   The following difficulties have been observed:

The aim of the Shop is to offer high quality professional services. This has led to most of the better paid jobs going to people from outside the area, creating some resentment from local people. There is however no programme to enable local people to gain the skills needed to take up the professional posts.

Solving Coping Or Preventing

3.3   *   The service focuses on "solving" counselling, i.e. in providing routes out of unemployment for people in the Greenvale area rather than in preventing unemployment. The Management Committee is philosophically and politically opposed to the notion of "coping". It believes there is potential for those who wish it to be able to advance their personal situation rather than to simply cope with it.

4.   **LESSONS TO BE LEARNED**

4.1   Community based initiatives in the control of local people can work.

4.2   Funding can often be available from the European Commission for such initiatives if they are supported by either central or local governments.

4.3   The image and reality of informality, independence, and confidentiality is attractive to the local people.

4.4   The Shop advertises its successes in the local paper. It is therefore seen to be providing a high value service to the community.

4.5   Some form of systematic follow-up is necessary to assess whether additional support services are needed for customers once they have gone through the Shop's initial counselling services.

European Foundation for the Improvement of Living and Working Conditions

Eurocounsel Synthesis Final Report Phase 2:
Counselling – a Tool for the Prevention and Solution of Unemployment

Luxembourg: Office for Official Publications of the European Communities

1994 – 130 pp. – 16 x 23.5 cm

ISBN 92-826-7868-7

Price (excluding VAT) in Luxembourg: ECU 13.50